A Journey Through Turbulence

Dignity Press
World Dignity University Press

"In his long career as a journalist and researcher, Deepak Tripathi has developed a deep understanding of the Middle East and South Asia during the Cold War, and America's place in the post-Soviet world. These essays, written at a critical time, make a very significant contribution, because they provide both an overview, and depth of knowledge, of current problems. This book should be widely read."

— GRACE FEUERVERGER, *professor of education, University of Toronto, and author of "Oasis of Dreams: Teaching and Learning Peace in a Jewish-Palestinian Village in Israel" and "Teaching, Learning and Other Miracles"*

"Tripathi writes with a degree of bite on the important issues of our times, covering the end of the Bush era to the start of Barack Obama's second term. These essays provide a searing commentary of U.S. foreign policy, and its failings from Iraq to Libya."

— DR. BINOY KAMPMARK, *RMIT University, Melbourne, and formerly Commonwealth Scholar, Selwyn College, Cambridge University*

"Lucid, imaginative, and intellectually independent, Tripathi provides a panoramic view of our recent turbulent history that is almost three dimensional. He has a rare ability to discuss historic events in a vast political landscape, without ever losing his central argument that war, humiliation, and injustice cannot bring peace. This book should be read by everyone."

— DR. EVELIN LINDNER, founder of the Human Dignity and Humiliation Studies Network, and professor of humanities and social sciences

"Deepak Tripathi gives scholars and activists alike an excellent understanding of what there is to know about what we know. He shows us whether our theory of knowledge comes from colonialism or universalism matters, and that this knowledge alone can help the peace process."

— RUTH O'BRIEN, *professor of political science, CUNY Graduate Center, and author of "Out of Many, One: Obama and the Third American Political Tradition"*

A Journey Through Turbulence

Writings of Deepak Tripathi

 Dignity Press
World Dignity University Press

Published by Dignity Press
16 Northview Court
Lake Oswego, OR 97035, USA

www.dignitypress.org
Book website: www.dignitypress.org/journey-through-turbulence

Cover photo: Desert Road, by avarooa - fotolia.com
Back cover photo: © Deepak Tripathi
Book design by Uli Spalthoff

Printed on paper from environmentally managed forestry:
www.lightningsource.com/chainofcustody

ISBN 978-1-937570-32-3
Also available as EPUB: ISBN 978-1-937570-33-0
and Kindle eBook: ISBN 978-1-937570-34-7

CONTENTS

CHAPTER THREE:
HUMILIATION AND RESISTANCE

CHAPTER FOUR:
GLOBALIZATION AND THE FALLOUT

CHAPTER FIVE:
HUMAN RIGHTS AND THE RULE OF LAW

FOREWORD

Deepak Tripathi has written a gripping account of the last decade of a falling empire, whose economic interests and cultural domination go hand in hand with militarism, creating ripple effects worldwide. The Journey Through Turbulence on which he skillfully takes the reader is a remarkably candid analysis of contemporary world affairs, from the point of view of a professional who allies his journalistic talent with the thoroughness of an academic experience. Deepak Tripathi's narrative of the last decade does not take the reader through a chronological account. Rather, its thematic compilations along the lines of aggression, humiliation, terror, but also hope, enable us to comprehend the various faces of the relationship between global North and South; as well as the social, political and economic dimensions of intra-national settings. The book takes us inside India, France, Pakistan, Greece, etc., without ever falling out of a larger international context.

A Journey Through Turbulence is written with the meticulousness of an acute observer of contemporary international relations. The book does not just connect the dots of a complex international picture. Every single article contains the elements that book represents as a whole. Like the zooming out of a fractal image, the reading of article after article uncovers a larger picture that asserts the reader in his conceptualization of world affairs through the last decade. From that perspective, Deepak Tripathi writes in a holographic manner, and the approach with which all the articles are joined together does justice to his dedication to allowing the reader to understand a turbulent world.

A classic Peace and Conflict Studies approach to conflict is to remind students that no one wakes up in the morning believing that he or she is a bad person. In this book, Deepak Tripathi vividly analyses the Bush era with the lens of a democracy going adrift. While no one can forget how Hitler was brought to power democratically in 1933, the book exposes how the Bush administration had managed to renegade on each and every one of America's ideals through so-called "War on Terror" induced actions. Extra-judicial killings, drone attacks, torture, the backing of tyrannies abroad for the sake of "saving one's country" are some of the many exactions that were carried out in the name of democracy. Witnessing the election of Barack Obama, Deepak Tripathi conveys the hope of a nation that resorts to elections to save its own soul, only to fall invariably into the structural traps of a country whose economy is based on war. The hope that the election of Barack Obama generated among many is soberly conveyed in this book, as if its author knew all along how this story would end for it domestically as well as for the rest of the world. Hope cannot cure a structural war-mongering machine, while at the same time it cannot cease to exist. Some gripping parts expose a lonely President Obama whose past closest allies seem to have deserted him, yet whose persona refuses to yield to the pessimism gripping his nation.

The form in which the book is written does not make concessions in front of the widespread human rights violations carried out across the world, this in the past decade, and regardless of a country's stand economically and politically. All throughout the book, Deepak Tripathi has sought to keep the individual as an important part of his writing, this due to his longstanding journalistic career. While it is so easy to be removed from the common life of people in academia, journalism seeks to retain a deep dimension of proximity to the human consequences of war and occupation. Close to my heart was the story of Mohammed Merah, from France, that of a young Muslim man who resorted to killing children and French army personnel who in his eyes embodied an oppressor. The Muslims who had joined the French army, which was deployed in Afghanistan at the time, were seen as infidels who needed to be punished, while the innocent Jewish children playing in their schoolyard before being gunned down in cold blood were supposed to represent the Israeli oppressor of Palestinians. It is with courage that Deepak Tripathi provides a context to the story of Mohammed Merah, and relates to the reasons that led him to murder, as well as his own summary execution by the French special police. As it has since become public knowledge that French intelligence had made a failed attempt to recruit him, and that this actually radicalized Mohammed Merah

to the point of committing the irreparable, Deepak Tripathi´s article
contextualizes this somber affair within an overall context of collateral
damage, resulting from a larger systemic conflict. In this sense, Mohammed Merah becomes another casualty of world politics, alongside his
civilian and military targets.

While the information of Merah´s failed recruitment by French intelligence, one of too many, was not available at the time that the article
was written, Deepak Tripathi´s professionalism enables his article to
stand the test of time in light of further evidence to the case. In this
sense, all the articles written in this book can claim to be equally relevant through time. This is due to the journalism and academic ethics
of a great writer who never finds himself carried away in the direction
of demagogical journalism.

I was delighted to be asked to write the foreword of A Journey Through
Turbulence as I have been keenly following the writing of Deepak Tripathi for many years. Over time, I have found myself increasingly moved
towards his work, as he became a significant reference in my academic
life. His analyses, approaches and conceptualizations of often-complex
situations have often provided the basis for my own writing on issues
that I was newly acquainted to. Similarly, when I had lost touch with
specific parts of the world, his articles allowed me to keep up to date
and engaged. Overall I think that the complexity that is always present in his works is a deep contribution to a balanced understanding of
world affairs. While objectivity in journalism and academia remains a
Cartesian myth, balance in monitoring the centers of power and their
impact on people´s lives is what ought to prevail in journalism today.
In that respect, Deepak Tripathi´s contribution to ethical and balanced
journalism makes him a life-long contributor to Peace Journalism as it
ought to be taught in Peace and Conflict Studies programs worldwide,
and practiced in mainstream journalism.

One cannot but end reading this book with a deep sense of hope that
the next decade of world affairs will not be as destructive as the last one,
with the optimism that lessons have been learned from systemic past
failures. This hope comes directly from the way in which all stories in
this book have retained a deep human touch that no doubt contributes
to a renewed call for a dignifying world. Deepak Tripathi´s effortless

practice of Peace Journalism reminds us that human dignity can be championed one article at a time, both as they are being written, and as they are being read. In reading this book, you will undoubtedly contribute to dignifying the world.

Victoria Fontan

Head, Department of Peace and Conflict Studies
UN-mandated University for Peace
San José, Costa Rica

Preface

After 23 years as a journalist, I had to retire from BBC News due to ill health in 2000. The future looked uncertain because suddenly I had to adapt to a different way of life after a hectic and eventful career. Fortunately, I had a deep interest in international affairs and acquired considerable experience during my working life of more than 25 years.

My travels were restricted, so I spent two years on a graduate study program in business administration of Heriot-Watt University in Scotland. Part of my study involved psychology and human relations, two of the subjects with applications in the wider world. I then spent five years (2002–2007) researching historical archives at the University of Sussex with concentration on Afghanistan and the Cold War. These had been among my interests since the 1970s, at the start of my career as a journalist, first in the United States and then in Britain. The result of my Cold War research was Breeding Ground (Potomac Books, Inc., 2011). It examined the multi-layered Afghan war in the 1980s and 1990s—a conflict far more vicious leading to more profound consequences than the ethnic war in Sri Lanka—the subject of my earlier book, Sri Lanka's foreign policy dilemmas (Royal Institute of International Affairs, Chatham House, 1989).

In early 2008, I had a new project. George W. Bush's presidency (2001–2009) was in its final phase and his "war on terror" had been going on for nearly as long as his presidency. The cost for the United States was enormous, no less for the rest of the world, in terms of loss of life and liberty. The world was hyper-polarized, the economy was heading for a crash. The social contract between the state and the individual was collapsing. Citizens' confidence in their leaders had sunk and hopelessness pervaded societies. As the German finance minister Peer Steinbruck remarked in an interview with Der Spiegel, "We are all staring into the abyss." The collapse of national economies in Greece, Italy, Spain and Ireland was about to occur.

I had been a correspondent and analyst for nearly a quarter century. My articles had appeared in the Economist and the Daily Telegraph of London in the 1990s. I had been a contributor to The World Today, monthly journal of the Royal Institute of International Affairs, Chatham House. After researching Cold War history from 2002 to 2007, I began to write for a broad range of periodicals on current topics of concern.

I am pleased that Dignity Press has decided to publish this collection of my writings during a particularly turbulent phase of contemporary history. The collection represents analyses of a broad range of events, organized around a number of themes. Taking a critical view, this book offers a panoramic picture of recent history with historical depth.

Deepak Tripathi
London, December 1, 2012

Chapter One:

The United States in the

Contemporary World

The Essence Of Patriotism

July 25, 2008

An election year in the United States guarantees a debate about patriotism, particularly when the country is at war. It is not a political discourse about a citizen's moral duty to do what they can to serve their country. I mean a debate in which patriotism is used as a weapon of attack in a brutish and nasty manner for character assassination, to depict a hitherto established politician as a dangerous or juvenile individual, who cannot be trusted with national security. Such tactics were deployed at their worst against Michael Dukakis in the 1988 presidential election by his Republican opponent, George H. W. Bush. His son, George W. Bush, the current incumbent in the White House, used the weapon of patriotism against John Kerry, whose notable war record was disparaged by the neoconservatives.

I have been an observer of U.S. politics for well over three decades. Experience tells me that the Republicans have an advantage in this nasty, brutish fight and are willing to deploy the weapon of patriotism ruthlessly against their opponents. In the election campaign that has barely started, there have been some bruising episodes in the Democratic nomination battle as well. I recall Hillary Clinton's warning that if the Iranian regime threatened Israel, she, as president, would obliterate the Iranian nation. I, a European, found the rhetoric frightening. Had President Ahmadinejad of Iran not used exactly the same kind of rhetoric, wishing that Israel was not on the map? So what was the difference? One meant to impress Iran's Shi'a population. The other America's Jewish voters and supporters of Israel. I do not believe either Ahmadinejad or Clinton was serious about obliterating any country. For they both know very well the consequences.

Hillary Clinton's more realistic, and calculated, aim was to make Barack Obama look weak. Now that the Democratic Party's nomination is settled, the electoral battle for the real prize, the White House, begins.

It is going to be more nasty. Questions about each candidate's experience, suitability and patriotism are going to be raised, accusations and counteraccusations will intensify, and so will personal attacks. When the stakes are high and the battle is fierce, chauvinism and intolerance are not far. I am struck by how narrow the meaning of patriotism can become in these situations. The recent visit of Barack Obama to Iraq is not surprising. Supporters of his Republican rival, John McCain, continue to focus on the question of patriotism and qualifications to be commander-in-chief of the United States. Why it should be so is, in part, because McCain's knowledge of the minutiae of the economy and international terrorism is poor.

It brings me to the meaning of patriotism. Is it McCain's assertion to keep American forces in Iraq for "a hundred years"? Or Obama's suggestion that, if elected, he would like to withdraw the American occupation forces from Iraq in 18 months, to concentrate on securing and rebuilding Afghanistan, which is rapidly sinking into the type of chaos that existed before the Taliban's removal from power after the September 11, 2001 attacks in New York and Washington? McCain displays a determination bereft of tact and sensitivity—qualities which the next American president will need. The Iraqi Prime Minister, Nouri al-Maliki, has recently made it plain that his government wants to see a date set for America's military withdrawal in the near future. Obama's position seems to be more nuanced, reflects more sensitivity and gives America room for maneuver. McCain, the old warrior, is locked in the mindset of Vietnam while Obama represents a generation that does not carry the same baggage.

Seven years after George W. Bush started his foreign adventure called "the war on terror," America shows a greater willingness to examine the journey it has undertaken and the trials and tribulations it has gone through. However, as a country, it still finds it difficult to disagree with its commander-in-chief, who is elected by the American people and who must be accountable to them. More than two hundred years ago, Thomas Jefferson, the third president of the United States, said something that is as true today as it was then. "Dissent," he said, "is the highest form of patriotism." And he went on, "The spirit of resistance to government is so valuable on certain occasions that I wish it to be always kept alive."

The spirit of dissent, fortunately, lives on more comfortably in Europe, even in Britain where Tony Blair, now ex-prime minister, was the closest ally of George W. Bush in the "war on terror." Even as he secured the British Parliament's approval to invade Iraq, as it turned out on a false premise, Blair could not succeed in creating groupthink—a condition in which a body of people accepts, and conforms to, prevailing points of view uncritically. Carl Schurz, German revolutionary, later American statesman and reformer, got it about right when he said, "My Country! When right, keep it right; when wrong, set it right!"

The maxim explains the difference between patriotism and jingoism, an outburst of extreme emotions that come out in the form of aggressive foreign policy.

THE STAKES IN THE 2008 U.S. ELECTIONS

September 26, 2008

"Nearly all men can stand adversity, but if you want to test a man's character, give him power," said Abraham Lincoln, the 16th president of the United States, almost 150 years ago. Today, the presidency of George W. Bush is in its twilight months. The season of presidential debates of 2008 has begun. America is in the midst of Palin-mania. Opinion polls predict a tight race between John McCain and Barack Obama. And I am reminded of the eternal truth spoken by Lincoln all those years ago.

The conduct of the Bush administration has affected the lives of countless people in America and around the world. As American voters approach polling day on November 4 to elect his successor, the outside world ponders with them. What have the last eight years been like? Where is America headed and what would it mean?

President George W. Bush was never a subtle politician. His personal charm and southern directness attracted many Americans and helped him win two elections for the White House. Each time, he also had a stroke of luck. The Bush victory in November 2000 was one of the most controversial, and disputed, presidential election results in the history of the United States. Just five electoral college votes separated him from his Democrat opponent, Al Gore. The state of Florida, with 25 electoral votes, gave that victory to Bush. Overall, Bush got half a million fewer popular votes than Al Gore, his defeated rival. The legal battle after the election went right up to the American Supreme Court, which decided that the recount of ballots by hand in Florida was unconstitutional and the Republican Secretary of State of Florida could certify the result.

The Florida vote count which gave George W. Bush the victory was so controversial because his brother, Jeb, was Governor there. The Secretary of State, Katherine Harris, who certified the Florida vote, was not only a member of Governor Jeb Bush's cabinet. She was also co-chairman of the presidential campaign of George W. Bush in the state. In the end, a majority of just 537 popular votes out of a total of nearly 6 million ballots cast in Florida decided the result. It was certified by a close ally of Bush and a recount by hand was declared unconstitutional in a U.S. Supreme Court dominated by conservative judges.

Four years later, it was his "war on terror" that, despite serious doubts, convinced America that it was not the time to reject an incumbent president. The 2004 presidential campaign was particularly nasty, just as the 2008 campaign is turning out. The neoconservatives, who ran the Bush campaign, focused on national security. Bush was projected as a decisive leader. His Democrat rival, John Kerry, was depicted as a "flip-flopper" by none other than the Vice President, Dick Cheney, to many the most powerful figure in the administration. One of Kerry's slogans "Strong at home, respected in the world" drew accusations that Kerry would pay more attention to domestic concerns, implying that defense would be ignored. Questions were raised about the legitimacy of the medals Kerry had been awarded during his military service in Vietnam. Bush had never fought in any war. But the 2004 Republican campaign was vicious. Kerry stood little chance. Today, John McCain, the Republican presidential candidate, lives in the glory of the Vietnam War, in which he endured abuse after capture and America lost. What was his achievement? The Republicans would not tell.

A president who has served eight years in office is bound to leave a legacy. The single issue that defines the legacy of George W. Bush is "the war on terror," pursued relentlessly during all but a few months of his presidency. It is tempting to suggest that the nature of American foreign policy under his administration was the consequence of the 9/11 attacks on the United States, but the explanation is simplistic. It provides no more than a convenient, and not entirely accurate, context to the "war on terror." In truth, the fundamental characteristic of the Bush presidency has been an uncomplicated view of the world and America's role in it. Behind the jingoistic frenzy, whipped up by the McCain-Palin ticket in the 2008 campaign, there is a much more profound question. What will a McCain-Palin administration, with an uncomplicated worldview and America's role, mean for the country and the world?

The retaliation against the Taliban and al Qaeda in Afghanistan after the September 11, 2001 attacks was understandable. But the scope of

American ambition under Bush was something else. The campaign to overthrow the Saddam Hussain regime in March 2003 on the basis of false claims that Iraq under him was developing weapons of mass destruction, the countless civilian deaths, the abduction, incarceration and abuse of tens of thousands of innocent people amount to crimes for which the leaders of many lesser countries would face trial. And it looked as though Iran and Syria would be the next targets in the "war on terror." Reckless threats of military action against Iran still continue. McCain and Palin may well carry on the same path, even though America remains bogged down in Afghanistan and Iraq.

The ideological vehicle used to get George W. Bush elected to the White House in November 2000 was the Project for the New American Century. By 2006, the organization seemed to have become inactive. However, a new band of Republicans aggressively pushing the same ideology has risen again in support of the McCain-Palin ticket. The old and discredited neoconservatives like Donald Rumsfeld, Paul Wolfowitz, John Bolton and Jeb Bush sought to link domestic controversies surrounding the Clinton administration to what they described as a drift in American foreign and defense policy in the 1990s. While domestic critics focused on the personal conduct of Bill and Hillary Clinton, the Project for the New American Century attacked the President's agenda for economic recovery. The implication was that Clinton's economic program had a cost in terms of weaker defense.

It is an irony that many enthusiastic supporters of Hillary Clinton, defeated in the Democratic nomination battle, should now contemplate switching to the McCain-Palin ticket. The message of the neoconservative constituency of George W. Bush was unmistakable—a more interventionist America, referring back to "Reaganite policy of military strength and moral clarity." But the ambition of the new right went further—"to build on the successes of the past century and to ensure our security and our greatness in the next." From the beginning, neoconservative associations like the Project for the New American Century believed that American power was absolute in its potential and that its use was inevitable. The language of McCain's running mate, Sarah Palin, echoes the same aggressive sentiment.

At this point, I want to discuss the general disposition of America's political right in recent years. In broad terms, it is an ideological movement representing a range of political and social organizations, which can be divided into two streams—neoconservatism and the religious right. The rise of the new conservatives in the late 1990s can be attributed to the rebirth of the coalition that came together under Ronald Reagan twenty years before. Many leading figures of the neoconservative movement were younger politicians and thinkers who had been out of power during the Clinton presidency. The other stream of the political right is religious.

There are significant differences in the American Christian right, ranging from Lutheranism and Catholicism to the more conservative Evangelical, Pentecostal and Fundamentalist Churches. White Evangelical voters account for more than 20 percent of the American electorate. Their overwhelming support for George W. Bush was largely responsible for his success in the two presidential elections. He received 68 percent of the white Evangelical vote in the 2000 election; it was 78 percent four years later.

There are differences, but there is also common ground, between those who make up the American political right. Differences are easier to identify on social issues. Moderate right-wingers tend to be less vehement in their opposition to abortion, stem cell research and homosexuals and less staunch in their support of the death penalty. At the other end of the religious right, there are those whose views on marriage, women's rights, abortion and homosexuality are extreme. One of the most controversial personalities of the religious right, preacher-politician Reverend Pat Robertson, has called feminism as a form of "socialist, anti-family political movement that encourages women to leave their husbands, kill their children, practice witchcraft, destroy capitalism and become lesbians." In 1998, Robertson claimed that acceptance of homosexuality could result in hurricanes, earthquakes and terrorist attacks. In the wake of the outcry after these remarks, he returned to the topic and, quoting from the Bible, sought to justify them.

Such demagogy, and attempts to resort to selective use of religious texts to legitimize extreme views, are not exclusive to the political right or left. Nor are they limited to the Christian right. We hear a lot about

Islamic fundamentalism, far less about Jewish, Hindu and Buddhist fundamentalisms. They, too, have been responsible for so much unrest in the Middle East, South Asia and other parts of the world. However, we must not lose the focus of discussion here. Our discussion is about the mass movement responsible for the presidency of George W. Bush.

Three main aspects characterize that movement. First, a strong belief in America's power and its right to exercise that ability. Second, a conviction in the superiority of Judeo-Christian values. And third, a strongly pro-Israel and anti-Muslim agenda. I referred earlier to the views of Pat Robertson, the preacher-politician. The rhetoric of another leading figure on the American right, Bill O'Reilly, is also worth mentioning. During a radio discussion about an opinion poll showing that most Iraqis did not see American troops as liberators and wanted them to leave the country, O'Reilly told listeners that he had "no respect" for the Iraqi people; they were a "pre-historic group" and the lesson from the Iraq War was for America not to intervene in the Muslim world again, but "bomb the living daylights out of them." His support for coercive techniques to extract information at detention centers such as Guantánamo Bay, trial in military tribunals and opposition to offering the detainees protection under the Geneva Conventions is well documented.

The rhetoric of people like Robertson and O'Reilly cannot be dismissed as irrelevant and unrepresentative. Both command huge audiences through their television and radio programs. Many aspects of the "war on terror" show the influence such views have had in the Bush administration. It is undoubtedly America's war. However, to bypass its obligations under the Geneva Conventions, the Bush administration invented a new concept of "enemy combatant" for detainees at Guantanamo Bay and other detention centers.

After sustained international criticisms and legal battles in the United States, the White House announced in July 2006 that it would comply with the third convention which guarantees the basic protection to detainees. The administration had no other choice after the U.S. Supreme Court ruled that the special military commissions set up to prosecute detainees violated U.S. law and the Geneva Conventions. It was a symbolic victory for opponents. Administration officials continued to argue about what really amounted to degrading and inhuman treatment, which is illegal under the fourth convention. The White House and the Pentagon maintained that the detainees were already treated humanely in the light of legislation passed in Congress barring "cruel, inhumane and degrading treatment" of detainees.

The overall disposition of the Bush administration since January 2001 reflects the instinctive belief across the new political right that American power is unlimited and unaccountable and the United States could decide unilaterally whether, when and to whom an international treaty would apply. The essence of such a mind-set is "we will do it because we can." In this respect, there is considerable unity of purpose across America's political right. It is driven by a domestic agenda. Foreign policy is an instrument to satisfy the conservative coalition at home for the sake of power.

As Americans approach polling day on November 4 to elect the next president, Lincoln's axiom assumes profound importance. Nearly all men can stand adversity and John McCain undoubtedly endured torture after being taken prisoner in Vietnam. That should not be the real issue, however. The real issue should be the character of the man who would be president—John McCain or Barack Obama. For, as Lincoln said, he is going to be tested by economic and foreign-policy problems unparalleled since America's withdrawal from Vietnam more than three decades ago.

POST-BUSH SCENARIOS

October 23, 2008

After war comes peace. With peace must come justice, or it will be meaningless. It is one of the most enduring lessons of history.

With the end of the Bush presidency in sight and the desire for change strong, the next president's inauguration on January 20, 2009 will be a turning-point. George W. Bush will retreat from the White House into retirement, leaving America exhausted, confused and polarized after eight years of foreign wars and domestic crises. His legacy will pass on to his successor. The conduct of the Bush administration has affected the lives of numerous people at home and abroad. As we approach something new and historic, a number of scenarios come to mind. The future not only depends on who will succeed Bush–John McCain, the old warrior, or Barack Obama, who increasingly looks like a renaissance man in the twenty-first century. It also depends on the nature of events to follow. They could force the hand of the incoming president.

Energy and the economy have become the main concerns in America and around the world. Seven years on, Americans, in growing numbers, have turned against the ideologues who manipulated fear to advance their own expansionist ambition. Americans want the next president to concentrate on rebuilding the economy and improving their lives. They remain conscious of the terrorist threat, but they are no longer willing to support foreign wars at great cost. The Bush-Cheney administration has tormented hundreds of millions of innocent people around the world in the "war on terror," although Afghans and Iraqis have borne the brunt. An unsettling realization has been building up among Americans of the extreme hardships and strong resentment this has caused abroad. It is time to make peace with the alienated and try to recover at least some of the wasted capital of sympathy the United States had earned immediately after the September 11, 2001 attacks. The Bush administration's wars are an expression of a mindset seriously infected with arrogance, reckless ambition and a passion for warfare, even against its own people.

What if, therefore, the next administration decided in favor of a rapid military withdrawal from Iraq to concentrate on the task of economic recovery? Iraq was invaded on a false pretext and against the advice of the U.N. weapons inspectors. Kofi Annan, then U.N. secretary-general, said the invasion was illegal. But a hasty retreat would be fatal, whether it was triggered by the new American president's desire to cut the losses, or because the Iraqi government told the U.S. occupation forces to leave. A swift withdrawal would leave the present Iraqi government more vulnerable and it might not survive. The Iraqi government is dominated by the Shi'a majority. Its relations with Iran are close. If the Iraqi government found itself in imminent danger, it would become even more dependent on Tehran.

The creation by the United States of 100,000-strong Sunni militia, described as the Awakening Council movement, evokes memories of the Mujahideen in Afghanistan, armed and financed by the CIA in the war against the Soviet Union in the 1980s. Until recently, many of these Sunni tribesmen belonged to al Qaeda. But they were lured with money and weapons by the Americans around 2006. In October 2008, America transferred the responsibility of paying their salaries to the Shi'a-dominated Iraqi government, which has strongly resisted pressure to incorporate them into the armed forces. If the militiamen were not paid in future, with or without the occupation forces being there in Iraq, they could change their uniform. They could just as easily turn against America and its allies as the Mujahideen did in Afghanistan at the end of the Cold War in 1991. The risks of what the Bush administration has done for short-term gains are huge.

The conflict in Iraq and the broader "war on terror" have brought great uncertainty to the region. They have contributed to the energy crisis and the worldwide economic slump. If the internal conflict in Iraq escalated again, the consequences would be catastrophic. The Iraqi state structure would be threatened. The military and the police, already fragile, would find that they are no match to a rebellious Awakening Council and other armed groups. Extreme caution would be required on the part of the incoming administration in Washington. A sudden, rapid withdrawal would involve great risks. So would the insistence on maintaining the U.S. military presence "for a hundred years," as John McCain said. It is obvious that the Iraqis do not want U.S. troops and the American economy cannot bear the drain caused by foreign military adventures. Withdrawal has to come, but the timing will be important. The next president must avoid a repeat of the 1990s Afghan scenario, total lawlessness and the rise of the Taliban, in Iraq.

We will have to wait and see whether the new president can show a capacity to relax a little and not be so obsessed with having client regimes everywhere. The persistent stubbornness of President Bush to reshape Afghanistan and Iraq in his own vision has been like pouring oil in fire. A perilous consequence of the Iraq war has been the neglect of Afghanistan. Seven years after the Taliban were removed from power, Kabul and other towns are under siege. It is a reminder of the period when Afghanistan was under Soviet occupation and Mujahideen guerrillas encircled the main population centers. The present conflict has spread throughout Pakistan and spilled over into India. Western experts admit the situation is spiraling out of control.

It would be refreshing if the next U.S. president decided that stability was more important than intervention to impose and maintain puppet regimes abroad. Instead of the edict of George W. Bush—"with us or against us"—his successor sometimes allowed governments to fall short of offering total support to America. The tendency to prop up dictators around the world was no longer rampant in Washington. There was a long-term strategy to encourage stability, not coercion to turn vulnerable nations into satellite states. The U.S. administration understood that war and economic renaissance could not happen together.

Conflict in the Middle East, high oil prices and economic downturns have had an unhappy relationship since the 1973 Arab-Israel war. Political turmoil and record energy prices have once again brought an economic slump with them. And the Palestinian problem, the main cause of the broader crisis in the region and beyond, remains unresolved. The urgent need to reduce America's dependence on Middle Eastern oil is at the center of the national debate. America has the necessary technological expertise and financial muscle to push for rapid progress towards alternative sources of energy, but its resolve has been weak since the 1973

Middle East war and subsequent oil crisis. Today, calls of 'Drill, Baby, Drill' may appear to provide short-term answers, but will play havoc with the environment. Their real cost would be very high.

Solar and fuel-cell energy technologies must be among tomorrow's solutions. Would the incoming president have what it takes to make America ready for a giant leap in a relatively short period? Would he take on the corporate world? Even if it turned out to be the case, I do not believe that the consequences of an energy revolution within a decade are fully appreciated. The impact of such a revolution on the oil-producing countries would be serious. To deprive them suddenly of their main—in many cases the only— source of income would be to leave them on the road to state failure. Saudi Arabia comes to mind immediately, but there are others in Asia and Africa. To make sure that they do not join the league of failed states, potential terrorist havens, would be as important for the successor of President George W. Bush as reducing America's dependence on foreign oil and rebuilding the economy.

A REVOLUTION TO REMEMBER

November 8, 2008

With the victory of Barack Obama in the 2008 presidential election, America has undergone a revolution. I say this not only for its symbolism, undeniable though it is. The entry into the White House of a president with black parentage is a powerful symbol—an event that has taken nearly two-and-a-half centuries since the American Revolution of 1776 and 150 years since the Thirteenth Amendment to the constitution outlawed slavery under the presidency of Abraham Lincoln in 1865. Progress of this magnitude is the end result of a monumental struggle, often by people whose names will not receive the limelight they deserve.

A revolution must go beyond such boundaries. It must be a wider response to critical problems in society, an acknowledgment by the masses that things have got to change, or there will be a greater calamity. Above all, a revolution is not a coup d'état which involves seizure of power by a small group of people. It is a wider phenomenon that happens when the time has come. The 2008 election in America reflects all of this and much more. The last eight years of the presidency of George W. Bush illustrate what damage can be done when the world's most powerful nation goes rogue, squandering its capacity to do good.

I belong to a generation born just after the Second World War. As someone who has lived and worked in America, travelled from coast to coast and one who has kept a keen eye on its politics, my interest in the country is abiding. With sadness, I say that I cannot recall a more repressive period in America's domestic and foreign affairs in my lifetime than the era that, I hope, will soon be behind us. It may sound uncomfortable to some, but the facts speak aloud.

At home, a mismanaged economy, driven down by hugely expensive foreign wars, crushing the middle-class America. The numbers of Americans struggling to stay above the poverty line are growing. In real terms, their plight invites comparisons with the basket cases in the

Third World: lack of food, nourishment, health care, education and job opportunities, security. Abroad, profound alienation from the United States, caused by the use of devastating military power by America and discredited client regimes. The scale of this repression has affected the lives of hundreds of millions of people. Such behavior loses friends and inflames armed opposition, leading to stronger retaliation. And the cycle goes on. The importance of prudence in the employment of power has never been greater.

The "war on terror," the project of the Bush presidency, has often made me think about something said by Mahatma Gandhi, who inspired leaders like Martin Luther King and Nelson Mandela. "What difference does it make to the dead, the orphans and the homeless," Gandhi said, "whether the mad destruction is wrought under the name of totalitarianism or the holy name of liberty and democracy?" Those who associate revolutions with the old-fashioned armed struggle in Russia or China in the first half of the twentieth century actually miss the point. A revolution is not necessarily a violent event. It is a definite and an overwhelming response against the existing order by people who feel they have had enough. This is what happened in America in 1776—the declaration of independence from Britain that Americans celebrate on July 4 every year. The abolition of slavery in 1865 was also a revolutionary event. So was the introduction of civil rights laws in the 1960s. In Europe, a number of Soviet bloc countries underwent peaceful "velvet revolutions" in the 1980s and 1990s.

The scenes all across America on November 4, 2008 were part of a phenomenon of profound magnitude. The turnout of more than 120 million people was unprecedented. An ocean of humanity pouring out, determined to vote, will be remembered for a long time. The margin of popular votes for Barack Obama was 52-46 percent—smaller than some opinion surveys had predicted, but still substantial. Obama's majority in the Electoral College, which actually elects the president, was 2-1. And the Democrats strengthened their hold by sizeable margins in both chambers of the U.S. Congress. The verdict was overwhelming.

Writing in Time magazine, Nancy Gibbs made the point that this victory was not achieved because of the color of Obama's skin, nor in spite of it. "He won because at a very dangerous moment in the life of a still young country," she said, "more people than have ever spoken before came together to try to save it." Her comments are all-encompassing. They tell the story of a superpower falling on hard times, nearly 20 years after it had defeated the Soviet Union in the Cold War, and thought that the capitalist system had won for good.

The scale of the Democratic victory in the 2008 election is a truly revolutionary event. But in the euphoria that prevails in America and, in many cases, beyond its shores, it would be prudent to introduce a note of caution. I know of no revolution fulfilling all that it promised. Americans have given their final verdict on the neoconservative order of the last eight years. It was an order which promoted a deregulated, free-for-all, corporate system and severe state controls on ordinary citizens at home and thoughtless militarism abroad; a form of state capitalism that made the Bush-Cheney administration the most unpopular in U.S. history. As a result, the economy is in turmoil, there is a crisis of faith in America and the country has suffered a loss of friendship and goodwill in the world.

The initial phase of the revolution is over. The old order has been rejected and the arduous task of fixing the broken system lies ahead. America has a total debt of 10 trillion dollars. Its budget deficit is likely to be more than 750 billion dollars when Obama takes over as president on January 20, 2009. As the recession deepens, hundreds of thousands of Americans are losing their jobs every month, while Europe and the rest of the world are dragged down. The Bush administration had chosen to fight three wars—in Afghanistan, Iraq and a global "war on terror." Dealing with these wars in the short run with a view to ending them eventually, hopefully before too long, is going to be a mammoth job. Fractured relationships abroad have to be rebuilt and engagement with international organizations must be revived. The most profound lesson of unilateralism of recent years is that the loss of international support for America weakens its leadership and makes it less effective in the world.

The most urgent task is economic revival, beginning with the restoration of the financial system. In the longer run, an enlightened approach to medical care, security and social welfare will be required to ensure the renaissance promised by the president America has just elected.

The number of people incarcerated in American prisons exceeds two million. At least five million more are on probation or parole—the vast majority of them from black and other ethnic minority groups. China, with four times the population of the United States, has fewer inmates in jail—around one-and-a-half million.

What is the total cost of all this and can anything be done? Consider the failure of the justice system which relies heavily on plea bargaining to secure convictions. The system convicts some of the most disadvantaged citizens, with little or no chance of proper legal representation. Consider, too, the lax gun laws and the violent incidents that lead to avoidable deaths and injuries and massive hospital bills. Two-thirds of Americans with insufficient medical cover or none at all. How many of the sick and the incarcerated die prematurely or spend their long years in prison, failing to contribute their best to America? These issues must be taken seriously in Washington. For without it, America is a failing state.

IMPERIAL AMERICA: SUCCESS OR FAILURE?

September 30, 2008

In a period of unprecedented financial upheaval, the recent surge in violence in South Asia is perhaps receiving less attention in the west than it deserves. The audacity of attacks by the Taliban and their al Qaeda allies in Pakistan and Afghanistan has implications for the region and beyond. The bombings of the Indian embassy in Kabul in June 2008 and the Marriott Hotel in Islamabad on September 20 have been devastating. Large swathes of Pakistan's frontier provide militant groups with sanctuaries, from where they launch attacks in both countries. The targets are chosen with precision and the campaign of violence has spread to India. A few days before the Islamabad bombing, a series of explosions in Delhi killed and maimed scores of shoppers at several locations. There have also been attacks in other Indian cities in recent months.

These events have caused tension between the Bush administration and Pakistan, America's main ally in the "war on terror." On more than one occasion, U.S. helicopters carrying troops have attempted to land inside Pakistani territory without authorization. Pakistani troops have fired on them and the helicopters have had to retreat. The anti-U.S. sentiment has rarely been so strong in the region. The authorities in Pakistan cannot afford to allow American troops on their soil. The authorities in India, with a Muslim minority nearly as large as the entire population of Pakistan, struggle to decide how far to move toward imposing draconian measures. How have things come to such a pass?

The origins of today's crisis rest in the past. For almost half a century after the Second World War, the United States had been at the forefront in efforts to contain communism. By December 1991, the Soviet empire had collapsed and America was in search of a new role. America's proxy war with the Soviet Union in Afghanistan had ended. Billions of dollars worth of weaponry was left in the devastated country. The strategic importance of Afghanistan had diminished for the United States. The army of Islamic groups, financed and equipped by America, turned bitter. In their eyes, it was a deliberate act of abandonment. The American economy had suffered years of decline, to which vast military expenditure on foreign wars had contributed. There were new opportunities to achieve economic renaissance at home and reshape the international order abroad. Bill Clinton, who won the presidency in November 1992, was keen to seize these opportunities.

However, there was a problem. Following the breakup of the Soviet state, Ukraine, Kazakhstan and Belarus had found themselves with almost all long-range nuclear weapons. Smaller tactical arms were scattered all over the territory of the defunct state. Every republic except Kyrgyzstan had inherited them. One nuclear state had suddenly become many. Unless these weapons were dismantled and Russia was helped to transform itself into a democracy in control of the ex-Soviet nuclear arsenal, the world would be a dangerous place.

When Clinton assumed the presidency in January 1993, America had already liberated Kuwait after brief Iraqi occupation. Clinton moved on to his agenda to stabilize the former USSR and rebuild the American economy. He was aware that a conservative takeover in Russia could start a new arms race and sink his plan for American renaissance. Clinton told his advisers to help Boris Yeltsin, the Russian president, in the transformation of his country. The focus of Clinton's policy was to be investment in Russia.

One of its consequences was a move from Afghanistan, left in a Hobbesian "state of nature"— war of all against all. The policy to rescue Russia continued until the end of the Clinton presidency. In the darkest period of Russia's economic crisis, Yeltsin was forced to default on repayment of foreign debt and devalue the Russian currency in 1998. Clinton pushed the International Monetary Fund to support a recovery program. Within two years, Russia's income from oil sales had risen substantially, helped by an increase in the world prices. The crisis had eased.

It was in the later part of 1994 that a little-known Islamic militia, described as the Taliban, came to prominence in southern Afghanistan, amid the destruction of what was left of the Afghan state. The country was split into numerous fiefdoms run by rival warlords. Afghan and foreign Mujahideen had spent years fighting the Soviet Union and its client regime in Kabul. Now, they had nothing to do. Foreign money had dried up. Weapons were plentiful and America had walked away. Murder, rape, looting and plundering became the way of life for these fighters, as Pakistan's rival agencies tolerated or collaborated with the Taliban to impose a brutal regime in Afghanistan. The civilian government of Benazir Bhutto in Pakistan and Saudi Arabia, the most important U.S. ally in the region, were the staunchest supporters of the Taliban regime, which gave sanctuary to al Qaeda. America had, in effect, handed over Afghanistan to Saudi Arabia, which represents the most totalitarian brand of Sunni Islam. Its junior partner was Pakistan.

The 9/11 attacks prompted the United States to return to Afghanistan to overthrow the Taliban regime and to destroy al Qaeda. Overthrowing the Taliban regime was the easy task, but the stabilization and reconstruction effort has suffered a calamitous failure. The Taliban and al Qaeda are regrouped and reinforced. Their top leaders continue to elude capture. Afghans at first welcomed their liberation from the Taliban. They are now very resentful of the Americans and their use of overwhelming force, resulting in large numbers of civilian casualties.

Afghanistan has been at the center of great power games for centuries. However, outsiders have always failed to tame the spirit of resistance of its people. At the peak of their dominance, the British and Russian empires played the Great Game. In the Cold War, it was between America and the Soviet Union. Today, as the United States, the only hyperpower in the world, tries to reshape the Afghan state, it finds the new game as difficult as ever. As the turbulent presidency of George W. Bush comes to a close, claims are heard about the "success" of America's military surge from the administration and the Republican presidential candidate, John McCain. There is talk of a similar surge in Afghanistan to suppress the violence by the Taliban and their allies. The factors behind the decline in violence in Iraq are many, including the fact that tens of thousands of Sunni tribesmen, erstwhile al Qaeda supporters, are now paid $300 a month each not to fight the occupation forces and the Shi'a-dominated government in Baghdad. Their alliance with America is tactical and temporary. Their long-term intentions are uncertain, especially if America withdraws or they are no longer paid. It all reminds me of the U.S.-Mujahideen alliance in Afghanistan before it fell apart almost 20 years ago.

The American military presence in Afghanistan today is about a third of the size of the Soviet occupation forces in the 1980s—a total of 120,000 soldiers. Many experts agree that the strength of the U.S. and NATO troops in Afghanistan is woefully inadequate and reinforcements are needed. But in the unique conditions of Afghanistan, it is much less certain that a surge there will bring lasting success. The battlefield now extends from the Gulf all the way to India. The problem requires a different solution involving regional powers, Iran and Syria included—an idea loathed by those who have been in power in recent years.

Obama's Foreign Crises

December 1, 2008

The carnage in Mumbai by young, well trained gunmen is the latest chapter in the world's most complex web of problems today. Not only is it bound to have new consequences, it also throws up fresh challenges for all concerned, not least for America's President-elect, Barack Obama.

When a bloodbath in India's main commercial center is played out on television screens across the world, people who have witnessed similar events in New York and Washington, London and Madrid, Islamabad and Bali immediately connect with a rapidly escalating phenomenon. India is no stranger to terror. Still, it has suffered a huge shock. The Indian economy, already caught up in a global recession, is bound to feel the impact. Tourism and investor confidence may suffer, at least in the short run. The political fallout may go beyond the resignation of the Home Minister, Shivraj Patil. The country faces a general election in May 2009. The governing coalition led by the Congress Party is under heavy criticism from the Hindu nationalists, as well as the population in general.

We have seen instances of backlash against Muslims in the United States and Europe after September 11, 2001. The Indian authorities will be mindful of this possibility in their own land. Violence against India's Muslim and Christian minorities has been on the increase. The authorities have come under criticism for failure to protect them. Fortunately, Islam has deep roots in India and the 150 million or so Indian Muslims were all born and brought up in a secular country. This does not, however, guarantee harmony between India's diverse communities. Opposition among Muslims against Indian rule in Kashmir, divided between India and Pakistan, has been a serious problem for the central government. Harsh measures by India's security forces to suppress the militancy fuel popular discontent even more.

As investigations continue into the massacre, there are accusations and counteraccusations within the governing coalition and between the opposition and the government. Relations between India and Pakistan have plunged following claims that the gunmen may have come by sea from Pakistan and belonged to a group based there. The attackers had AK-47 assault rifles manufactured in abundance on the western frontier of Pakistan, where Taliban and al Qaeda have sanctuaries and training camps. The sustained ruthlessness and cold-blooded determination of the gunmen to kill until the end was a product of a hardened, well-trained frame of mind.

The president-elect of the United states, Barack Obama, had made the economy his number one priority upon taking office in January 2009. With the recent events in India, he faces another big challenge. Claims of improvement in Iraq are no longer enough to reduce America's engagement in the Middle East and concentrate instead on the Afghan theater and rebuild the U.S. economy. The truth is that the web of crises spans from Palestine through Iraq, Afghanistan and Pakistan to India and further east. The combination of extreme remedies applied as part of the "war on terror" and neglect of the real issue in the Middle East, the Palestinian crisis, by the outgoing Bush administration has added fuel to the fire. Mistakes have alienated many decent ordinary people. Same old condemnations of "uncivilized terrorists" and perfunctory support for their victims seem increasingly meaningless.

A strong sense of alienation, humiliation and injustice pervades the Middle East and South Asia. When the situation is volatile, local crises feed each other until they become a catastrophe. The chain of events illustrates the way in which many problems have become one. One-and-a-half million Palestinians remain cut off in the Gaza Strip, virtually imprisoned without sufficient food, fuel and medicine. More than a million of them are registered as refugees with the United Nations. They rely on humanitarian assistance that cannot be distributed as it should. The blockade of Gaza may be aimed at breaking the will of its people to support Hamas, which won the parliamentary elections for the Palestinian Authority in 2006, but the embargo has had the opposite effect. The conditions in the territory are increasingly desperate and desperate people resort to desperate measures. Underground tunnels have been dug in to Egypt to secure access to essential goods. The humanitarian situation demands urgent and extraordinary remedies to prevent the one-and-a-half million residents of the territory reaching the point where desperation is beyond containment.

The Palestinian problem is central to the wider crisis in West and South Asia. Its solution requires historic efforts involving America and Russia, as well as regional powers including Syria, Iran, Turkey, Egypt, Saudi Arabia, Pakistan, India and China. Obama has repeatedly offered friendship and support to Israel—a political necessity for any successful American politician. The time has come to exercise a restraining influence on the Israelis. The president-elect says he is willing to negotiate with Iran, which has a nuclear program. In Afghanistan and Pakistan, the United States already conducts discreet negotiations with the Taliban. Israel does the same with Syria. In the light of these overtures, the refusal to hold talks with Hamas does not make sense.

The rest comes after the Palestinian problem. Following prolonged negotiations, the timetable for America's military withdrawal from Iraq is set. It is to be completed by the end of 2011, provided unforeseen events do not frustrate the plan. For the success in stabilizing both Iraq and Afghanistan, Iran's cooperation is essential, but the more hawkish the U.S. administration becomes, the less chance there is of securing that vital support. At the same time, cooperation of Syria, another big player in the Middle East, is essential for progress in Lebanon and elsewhere.

The crisis across the triangle that includes Afghanistan, Pakistan and India has both distinct and common aspects. The Taliban are an indigenous tribal movement across the Afghanistan-Pakistan frontier and cannot be eliminated. However, it is possible to influence them if conditions are right in both countries and Washington shows willingness to listen to regional experts. America has been heavily involved in both Afghanistan and Pakistan for almost three decades. It played a role in the war. Now it needs to play a part in their reconstruction and stabilization in the interests of all. Last but not least is Kashmir, a territory disputed between India and Pakistan since their independence from Britain in 1947. The prospects of a resolution to this intractable problem could improve with democratic reforms in Pakistan and with America's engagement with Pakistan's civilian political establishment instead of military. Reforms are also needed on the Indian side of Kashmir, where a combination of political failures and heavy-handed military tactics over many years has fuelled popular disaffection and strengthened the militants.

A DIALOGUE FOR RECONCILIATION?

June 5, 2009

The upheaval in America's relations with the Muslim world after September 11, 2001, as well as its content and language, make the eagerly-awaited address by President Obama in Cairo on June 4 an event of significance. Speculation in recent weeks had focused on how different Obama's message would be from that of his predecessor, George W. Bush. That it would be different was not in doubt. Obama had spoken of the unclenched fist meeting the extended hand soon after his inauguration as president. Recent speculation had centered on that vision and its detail. Those expecting were not disappointed. The reaction fills the spectrum of opinion.

A revolutionary speech has several essential qualities. It must address major problems of the day and generate widespread interest. It must inspire hope and be a pointer to long-term solutions. A revolutionary speech touches the lives of ordinary people, effortlessly overcomes ethnic, racial, religious divides; its call is for fairness and justice; it must be without extreme language; the time and the place have to be right.

President Obama's address in Cairo addressed two of the biggest problems of our time. One, the Israeli-Arab dispute, at the heart of which is Israel's festering conflict with the Palestinians. The other, the estrangement of Muslims that has grown to frightening proportions, no less due to the "clash of civilizations" theory that had found abode in the Bush White House. These two problems, one caused by a historic injustice, the other of George W. Bush's own making, have affected the lives and thinking of Muslims round the world. Progress is unthinkable without addressing them.

Obama seems to have a gift of rhetoric full of inspiration and sympathy for the underdog, as well as evenhandedness, that his predecessor never had. The right sentiment conveyed in an appropriate language matters. Armed with knowledge of history, he paid tribute to the Egyptian civilization, particularly the place Al-Azhar University has in Islamic learning. And he was careful to put Islam at the same par as Christianity and Judaism, the other two great religions that have coexisted in the region for more than two millennia. He gave the speech in the most significant Arab country and, without going to Israel, travelled to Germany to visit the Nazi camp at Buchenwald, where more than 50,000 Jews, gypsies, resistance fighters and other prisoners were murdered.

To speak the word "occupation" for conditions in which Palestinians live in Gaza and the West Bank is a remarkable departure for an American president. Obama further described the situation of Palestinians as "intolerable." He spoke of tensions fed by colonialism that "denied rights and opportunities to many Muslims." And a Cold War in which Muslim-majority countries were too often treated "as proxies without regard to their own aspirations." He referred to the reinforcement of American troops in Afghanistan, but he also said that America did not want to keep its troops in that country. These words are powerful enough to resonate, not only in the Middle East, but also in distant lands.

Obama said he was in Cairo to seek "a new beginning between the United States and Muslims" around the world, one based "on mutual interest and mutual respect." While expressing Washington's traditional support for Israel, calling the bond unbreakable, he said, "It is also undeniable that the Palestinian people, Christians and Muslims, have suffered in pursuit of a homeland." Their daily humiliations are real. Then came perhaps the most significant part of his address: "America will not turn our backs on the legitimate Palestinian aspiration for dignity, opportunity and a state of their own."

The power of the Israel lobby in Washington, especially its dominance in Congress, remains strong, but outside Capitol Hill, the political landscape has changed. Depending on the perspective from which it is viewed, Barack Hussein Obama both leads and follows the extraordinary momentum of today. Obama's speech in Cairo has caused shockwaves in Israel's ruling establishment. In a muted response, the Israeli government said that national security will always be paramount for it. We are heading for extraordinary diplomatic turbulence, and many are eager and waiting to find out what comes after this turbulence.

COMPROMIZED DOMESTIC POLICY, MILITARIZED FOREIGN POLICY

December 29, 2009

With President Obama about to complete his first year in office, it is appropriate to look at the recent past and what may lie ahead. For the Obama presidency, it has been more of a downhill journey than a steep climb that many of his supporters and admirers in America and around the world had expected. President Obama will miss the January 22 deadline he set himself a year ago to close the Guantanamo Bay prison camp. As the New York Times recently pointed out, difficulties in finding places abroad to resettle prisoners deemed innocent and Congressional resistance to approving money to transfer high-security terrorism suspects to a special prison in Illinois have made it impossible to meet the deadline.

Obama's healthcare reform bill has had an arduous passage in the U.S. Congress. After a long battle, the House of Representatives finally approved its version including a government-run healthcare option the president wanted. It was a different matter in the Senate, where a filibuster-proof 60-vote majority could only be secured when Senate Democratic majority leader Harry Reid dropped the government insurance option to ensure support from conservative Democrats. Not one Republican senator backed the bill. And Reid and the House Speaker Nancy Pelosi were forced to concede on other major issues, including restrictions on abortion coverage.

These concessions have infuriated liberals. One of the disappointed is Obama's personal physician of 22 years, Dr. David Scheiner, who does not believe the planned overhaul goes far enough to help the poor and uninsured, and will cost too much. Dr. Scheiner, bitterly disappointed, said he was excluded from the list of invitees to the White House under pressure from the health lobby. Even so, President Obama congratulated the Senate, and by implication himself, on its historic vote, proclaiming that "we are now finally poised to deliver on the promise of real, meaningful health insurance reform."

Compare the content and tone of President Obama's remarks at his inauguration, his Cairo address to the Muslim world in June and his Oslo speech accepting the Nobel Peace Prize in December 2009. Couched in the familiar rhetoric is increasing aggression and militarization of American foreign policy of the Obama presidency. The inauguration speech included remarks about the United State being a nation of Christians and Muslims, Jews and Hindus, and nonbelievers; a message to the Muslim world that America sought a new way forward, based on mutual interests and mutual respect; and a warning to those who cling to power through corruption and deceit.

In Cairo, Obama acknowledged tensions between the United States and Muslims around the world, not only rooted in historical forces, but also fed by colonialism that denied rights and opportunities to many Muslims; and a cold war in which Muslim-majority countries were treated as proxies without regard for their aspirations. Reaction from the Muslim world and outside was generally positive. The speech was seen as a possible new beginning after the three-week Israeli war on Gaza that took the lives of 1,400 Palestinians in comparison to 13 deaths on the Israeli side during the last days of George W. Bush's presidency in December 2008/January 2009.

In a surprise but divisive move, the Nobel Committee announced the award of the 2009 Peace Prize to President Obama for his "extraordinary efforts to strengthen international diplomacy and cooperation between peoples." Soon, the Nobel Committee's announcement began to look like a triumph of hope over reality. In early December, after weeks of deliberations, he announced before a uniformed audience at the West Point military academy, "As commander-in-chief, I have determined that it is in our vital national interest to send an additional 30,000 U.S. troops to Afghanistan." It reminded of speeches made by George W. Bush during his "war on terror."

Within days, Obama administration officials overturned the president's July 2011 deadline for starting a withdrawal stipulated in his speech. Sitting with Secretary of State Clinton and Joint Chiefs Chairman

Admiral Mullen, Defense Secretary Gates said 3,000 more troops could be needed on top of that. Britain and other allies announced smaller increases—all taking the Afghan surge to 40,000 troops or over. The war vision of America's military complex projected in General McChrystal's report was being implemented.

For all his expressions of gratitude and humility, Obama's acceptance speech at the Nobel award ceremony was an awkward one for the occasion. Once the almost obligatory references to figures like Martin Luther King and Nelson Mandela were out of the way, Obama quickly reminded the world that he was the commander-in-chief of the United States. He invoked the concept of a "just war" which is waged as a last resort, and in which force is used in proportion and civilian lives are spared whenever possible. In a convincingly argued, if provocative, article titled "Obama's Af-Pak War is Illegal," U.S. law professor Marjorie Cohn tackled Obama's claims about America's war in Afghanistan being a "just war" and found those claims wanting. Cohn pointed out that many Congressional Democrats were uncomfortable with Obama's decision and called on them to hold firm, even refusing to fund the war. A deep sense of disappointment and anger had spread among liberal and progressive supporters who had staked a lot in an Obama victory bringing a real change. But change is not the word much in use in the Obama rhetoric any longer.

The increase in U.S. drone attacks inside Pakistan's territory and the resulting casualties including old people, women and children fuel anger and resentment among local tribal communities and the country's intelligentsia. As CNN's Peter Bergen said in his analysis at the end of October, a Gallup poll showed only 9 percent of Pakistanis supported the strikes against two-thirds who opposed. According to UN human rights investigator Philip Alston, drone strikes causing civilian deaths may well violate international law. Newsweek's Mark Hosenball wrote that while some counterterrorism officials in the Obama administration wanted to expand drone operations to Pakistani cities, one person standing in the way of expanded strikes was President Obama.

The president's first year in office reveals limitations of his original thinking behind the formation of, in effect, a coalition administration. It includes President George W. Bush's defense secretary, Robert Gates, and Obama's onetime rival for the Democratic nomination, secretary of state Hillary Clinton, who had threatened to obliterate Iran if it attacked Israel with nuclear weapons, which Iran did not have. Candidate Obama had accused her of echoing the "bluster" of then president George W. Bush. On the military command side, two counterinsurgency hawks of the Bush presidency, General David Petraeus and General Stanley McChrystal, remain in command of America's war. The immediate future does not look bright.

HEADING FOR A HOLLOW VICTORY

September 26, 2012

We have run into greater turbulence following the appearance in the United States of a blasphemous film, Innocence of Muslims, about the Prophet Mohammad. The film was supposed to have been made by a convicted fraudster living in California, Nakoula Basseley Nakoula, and was promoted by Florida Pastor Terry Jones, previously involved in the burning of the Quran. That the causes of turmoil lie closer to us may be too unpalatable to accept for many in Western societies, but sadly it is true. When passions run high and it is difficult to see clearly, calm reflection, not ritual condemnation, is preferable. As the thirteenth-century mystic poet and theologian Jalaluddin Rumi wrote, then is time to "close both eyes to see with the other eye."

In the age of ceaseless electioneering, America's domestic politics determine its behavior abroad, and leave little scope for reflection on anything other than votes and power. This major fault line in the American political system gives extremist individuals and fringe groups a voice far louder than their size would suggest. Their capacity to radicalize the population is significant. They push some moderate figures seeking power to take more extreme positions. Other voices are muted for fear of damaging their political careers. What happens in America thus affects the rest of the world. This phenomenon is unsustainable, but will continue wreaking havoc for as long as it lasts. Islamophobia does exist in Europe, too, but the scale of Christian fundamentalism and the anti-Islamic sentiment in the United States is quite different.

A decade after the United States launched its hegemonic venture under the "war on terror" banner, Washington faces an unprecedented challenge to its authority in the Middle East and beyond. The assassination of the American ambassador Christopher Stevens in Benghazi, and attacks on Western embassies in other places, are difficult to explain away simply by apportioning blame on a few Muslim extremists. That open hostility expressed by violent means involves relatively small crowds is not in dispute. The more important and worrying aspect of the anti-U.S. protests is their worldwide dimension, and the depth of disapproval of America's conduct by moderate Muslims and non-Muslims alike. A Pew survey of global attitudes published in June 2012 shows a collapse in support for the Obama administration's international policies, even in Europe and Japan.

The message from the rest of the world to Obama on his drone attacks and his "Kill List" is stark. Of 20 countries where people were asked, only in two there were more respondents who approved killing by drones than those who disapproved. Those countries were the United States and India. According to Pew, there remains a widespread perception that the United States acts unilaterally and does not consider the interests of other countries. On one hand, many think America's economic clout is in decline. On the other, people around the globe overwhelmingly oppose the way the United States uses its military power in international affairs. They include people in Germany, France, Italy, Poland and Japan. As Obama fights to win in November his second and final term against a bumbling Republican opponent Mitt Romney, Washington's credibility and moral standing are sinking. It is this trend which perhaps explains the strength of challenge to America's authority more than anything else.

Another investigation, this time by academics of Stanford and New York universities, puts the blame on President Obama for the escalation of CIA drone attacks in which groups are selected by remote analysis of "pattern of life." The "dominant narrative about the use of drones in Pakistan is of a surgically precise and effective tool that makes the US safer by enabling 'targeted killings' of terrorists." But the report concludes that "this narrative is false." The number of 'high-level' militants as a percentage of total casualties is only about 2% of [deaths]. "The US practice of striking one area multiple times, and evidence that it has killed rescuers, makes both community members and humanitarian workers afraid or unwilling to assist injured victims." Residents in remote tribal areas across the Pakistan-Afghanistan frontier are "afraid to attend weddings and funerals."

Developments such as these provide the logic of popular antagonism against the United States across continents. A decade on, the "war on terror" has extended far beyond the Taliban and al Qaeda. As America prepares for a retreat from Afghanistan, NATO troops in that country live in fear not only of the enemy, but Afghans who were supposed to be their allies. Antagonists who challenge the United States come from many sections of populations in Africa, the Middle East, Asia and Europe. They are both militants and moderates who may not see eye to eye with each other on tactics, but their goals are similar. The stakes are high, the prospects gloomy. Barack Obama, a prisoner of forces that have historically ruled America, is unlikely to heed the message from the wider world for as long as he is in the White House. Unlikely, too, is the prospect of the anti-U.S. tide turning.

CHAPTER TWO:

AGGRESSION AND WAR

THE AXIS OF EVIL AND THE GREAT SATAN

September 8, 2009

"America is the Great Satan, the wounded snake."
—Ayatollah Khomeini, November 5, 1979

"States like [Iran, Iraq, North Korea] constitute an axis of evil,
arming to threaten the peace of the world."
—President George W. Bush, January 29, 2002

Spoken two decades apart, these words sum up the troubled history of the relationship between Iran and the United States. The German philosopher, Friedrich Nietzsche, once said, "There are no facts, only interpretations." His observation holds true about the manner in which Tehran and Washington remain preoccupied with each other. No significant event in Iran can go without repercussions for relations with the West. Almost 30 years after the overthrow of Iran's autocratic ruler and America's policeman in the oil-rich Gulf, Mohammad Reza Shah Pahlavi, the legacy continues to haunt both countries.

The presidential election of June 2009 in Iran was no exception. Mahmoud Ahmadinejad, the conservative incumbent, was seeking reelection after four turbulent years. A range of internal and external peculiarities surrounded the campaign that was exciting as well as unique. In a country of 72 million people, two-thirds are under 30 years of age and the rate of literacy exceeds 75 percent. Iran's economy has suffered a steady decline. Oil revenues have failed to benefit the population. The downturn in the world economy has affected Iranian oil exports particularly hard, and its balance of payments difficulties are acute due to low financial reserves.

Inflation was over 30 percent during the summer of 2008, when the Central Bank intervened to limit lending to prevent the resulting expansion of the money supply. In 2009, inflation has come down but has still been around 24 percent. Unemployment is 17 percent, about a third higher than 2005, when Ahmadinejad first became president. The chorus of criticism of Ahmadinejad for economic mismanagement grew as the election drew near, not only from his political opponents but sometimes from his one-time supporters. The Islamic Revolution Devotees Society, a fundamentalist grouping of revolutionary veterans cofounded by the Iranian President himself, accused him for starting huge state-funded projects while Iran's poor suffered and his stated goal of social justice was undermined.

Ahmadinejad routinely dismisses such complaints, saying that they are a product of intervention by hostile media. He blames "secret networks" for rising house prices. He has a doctorate in engineering, but often makes light of complaints about the economy by telling jokes. He told Iranian MPs to visit his grocer to find out the truth about the rising price of tomatoes. He suggests that he often takes advice about the economy from his local butcher, who knows about the economic problems of the people. And he says that he prays to God he never learned about economics.

The electoral system of Iran is by no means perfect, but not as bad as in some other countries in the region. In Saudi Arabia, small Gulf emirates and Egypt, elections are either nonexistent or held under extreme restrictions. Rigging is widespread in these states ruled by America's allies. In the June 2009 presidential election, Ahmadinejad, the incumbent, faced three challengers. Mir-Hossein Mousavi was seen as the leading challenger. He was Iran's last prime minister (1981-1989) before a presidential form of government was introduced. Three others had been rejected by the Council of Guardians, which vets all candidates. Former President, Mohammad Khatami, a liberal in the context of Iran, announced his candidacy but later withdrew and declared his support for Mousavi. Another ex-President, Ali Akbar Hashemi Rafsanjani, often described as a centrist-pragmatic conservative, was also known to be unhappy with the state of affairs.

The high percentage of young voters, economic decline and restless-ness among influential Iranians encouraged many inside and outside Iran to believe that the time was ripe for political change. President Obama's Cairo speech, seeking "a new beginning between the United States and Muslims," came a few days before polling day in Iran. His words of reconciliation were a source of new hope for moderates and liberals in the country. They enlivened the prospect for improvement in U.S.-Iran relations, perhaps for the first time since the 1979 revolution.

In the end, Ahmadinejad was declared reelected by a two-thirds majority, primarily because voters in the Iranian countryside did not abandon him. After an exciting campaign, sharp exchanges between candidates during television debates and overly optimistic reports in the foreign press, it was a bitter disappointment for Iran's opposition. Its supporters came out in large numbers in cities in towns, but their protests did not grow to a popular revolution. The coercive instruments of the Iranian state, the military, the intelligence services and police, remained intact. A crackdown on opposition supporters followed. For a while, there were loud protests in America from the Republican right, the Israel lobby and human rights groups. They only played into the hands of the religious hardliners in Tehran, and the liberal opposition of Iran found itself isolated even more.

Relations between Washington and Tehran sank to a new low follow-ing the events of 9/11 and Bush's description of Iran as part of the "Axis of Evil." Two factors in particular came to the fore: Iran's nuclear program, assisted by America and its allies when Mohammad Reza Shah Pahlavi, Washington's ally, was Iran's ruler; and accusations of Iranian support for international terrorism. In a leaked letter obtained by Associated Press in September 2006, the International Atomic Energy Agency described as "outrageous and dishonest" claims made in a report by the U.S. House of Representatives Intelligence Committee that Iran's nuclear program was geared towards making weapons.

The IAEA letter described the report to be "false in saying that Iran is making weapons-grade uranium at an experimental enrichment site." In fact, the agency said, the material produced was only in small quantities far below that can be used in nuclear weapons. The clash between Wash-ington and IAEA experts was reminiscent of earlier disputes between them over whether President Saddam Hussein was involved in developing weapons of mass destruction. Those claims in Washington and London were given as the principal reason for the invasion of Iraq in 2003. The claims were subsequently discredited when no traces of weapons of mass destruction were found. However, it did not prevent the Bush administration from using similar tactics against Iran, with the United States and Israel issuing warnings that Iran's nuclear research facilities might be bombed.

The failure of the U.S.-led invasion forces to produce evidence was one factor that conspired against an attack on Iran. Another was the outbreak of full-scale war following the dissolution of the Iraqi state structure by Paul Bremer, head of the American-led occupation authority. The conflict in Iraq defied the Bush administration's calculations and prevented the Americans from using strong-arm tactics against other adversaries. Diplomatic pressure and threats, however, continue even after the Bush presidency.

On September 7, 2009, the IAEA Director General, Mohamed El-Baradei, delivered his last report to the Board of Governors, two months before his retirement. He said that although Iran had "cooperated with the agency on some issues," several critical areas remained "unaddressed." Iran had not suspended its enrichment-related activities or its heavy water-related project, as required by the UN Security Council. Choosing his words carefully, El-Baradei said that these issues needed to be clarified "in order to exclude the possibility of there being military dimensions" to Iran's nuclear program.

President Ahmadinejad has by now ruled out further concessions by Iran. He recently told journalists in Tehran, "From our point of view, Iran's nuclear issue is over. We will never negotiate over the obvious rights of the Iranian nation." Tehran has also accused Washington of faking intelligence reports suggesting that Iran has "studied ways to make atomic bombs." Press TV, Iran's state-funded channel, quoted officials saying the United States had not "shared the original documents" it claimed to have a year ago, and there is no credible evidence of Iran pursuing a nuclear weapons program.

The outgoing IAEA Director General, Mohamed El-Baradei, is also highly critical of the West and its allies, France and Israel in particular.

Both have accused El-Baradei of "suppressing damning evidence" of Iranian attempts to build nuclear weapons. To them, the IAEA chief said, "I am dismayed by the allegations … which have been fed to the media that information has been withheld from the Board. These allegations are politically motivated and totally baseless." He bitterly complained that such attempts to influence the work of the IAEA Secretariat and undermine its independence and objectivity are in violation … of the IAEA Statute and should cease forthwith.

As El-Baradei prepares to retire, accusations and counteraccusations continue to fly between all concerned parties. There exists a stalemate over the nuclear issue, and the United States and Iran remain engaged in a game of brinkmanship.

Afghanistan And Presidential Dilemmas

November 13, 2009

News that the U.S. ambassador to Kabul, Karl Eikenberry, has sent classified messages to Washington, advising President Obama not to send more troops to Afghanistan, is dramatic both in its timing and substance. It came just as Obama was to hold further deliberations with his advisers on a new strategy for what is now described in Washington as the Af-Pak front. The substance of Eikenberry's advice went directly against the plan the military commander in Afghanistan, General McChrystal, has been pushing for in recent months. Eikenberry's intervention is highly significant. A Harvard and Stanford-educated general, he had served in Afghanistan twice before retiring and was immediately appointed America's envoy in that country in April 2009. He has strong military credentials and President Obama's ear—an effective counter to the Pentagon lobbying for ever-increasing military commitment to the war.

The contrary advice from Eikenberry may have annoyed General McChrystal, but represents an established pattern by now. Well orchestrated media reports originating from advocates of greater American involvement before every new strategy session, apparently intended to bounce the president into sending more troops; and President Obama finding a way to resist that pressure. Whatever criticisms are leveled against Obama over his perceived hesitation or dithering, these maneuvers within the administration point to his dilemmas. For unlike George W. Bush, an instinctive demolisher, Obama is in comparison more averse to war.

The last two decades of the twentieth century were a period of exceptional savagery in Afghanistan. First, it was committed during Soviet occupation and the U.S.-Soviet proxy war in the 1980s. Then came the West's neglect of Afghanistan and the outbreak of a "war of all against all" following the collapse of Soviet and Afghan communism. The culture

of violence to which powers great and small and Afghan factions themselves contributed became deeply ingrained in Afghan society. Violent
human behavior was revealed in more frightening ways than before.

The opening decade of the new century brought the horror of 9/11
early. Its conclusion reminds us of the Soviet decade in Afghanistan and
the American military era in Vietnam before the 1975 withdrawal. In
2009, the total strength of American and allied troops in Afghanistan is
more than 100,000, nearly as high as the number of Soviet troops two
decades before. Already, it has become the bloodiest year for the U.S.-
led international forces, with numerous civilian deaths in Afghanistan
and Pakistan. And General McChrystal wants 40,000 extra soldiers,
warning his commander-in-chief that otherwise the mission would fail.

In his August 2009 report, General McChrystal presented to the
Obama administration a list of "new objectives" in Afghanistan. Among
them are: "discredit and diminish insurgent and their extremist allies'
capability"; "promote the capability of, and confidence in, the Afghan
National Security Forces"; and "maintain and increase international
and public support for ISAF goal and policies" in Afghanistan. Those
keeping a keen eye on the conflict might ask what has the international
occupation force been doing for 8 years and what is new in McChrystal's
objectives? His assessment further says that the international force has
not adequately been executing the basics of counterinsurgency warfare.
So more military (with civilian) resources must be committed.

General McChrystal's remedy bears a striking resemblance to a letter written by Colonel K. Tsagolov of the Soviet military to his defense
minister Dmitry Yazov in August 1987. At a time when the Soviet
leader Mikhail Gorbachev had decided to withdraw from Afghanistan after a failed invasion and occupation, Colonel Tsagolov, using
Marxist jargon, wrote, "A deep political crisis of the Afghan society is
obvious…The coalition of social forces continues to change in favor of
the counter-revolution. The state regime is not capable of stopping the
counterrevolution on its own."

Colonel Tsagolov criticized the policy of national reconciliation being
pursued by the then president, Najibullah, at the Kremlin's behest.
Tsagolov observed that "our efforts over the last eight years have not
led to the expected results"; national reconciliation "has not led to a

breakthrough in the military-political situation, and will not lead to one." The "counter-revolution will not be satisfied with partial power today, knowing that tomorrow it can have it all." Colonel Tsagolov's recommended solution was to "help the progressive political forces" to preserve the "democratic content" of the country; and to "ensure future development of social processes" in Afghanistan "in the direction of our long-term interests."

How did the US/ NATO war in Afghanistan become so brutal, falsifying the first impressions in the wake of an "easy victory" in overthrowing the Taliban regime? From the outset, one side in the new Afghan conflict has had overwhelming power and acquired impudence. But the underdog has had strength in numbers, prepared to make the ultimate sacrifice. Fear has lost its deterrent quality. Death is no more an unwelcome prospect. Life has to be endured, not enjoyed. And the rationality in martyrdom has replaced the rationality in survival among those who fight the occupation forces. Human beings are at their most dangerous when they no longer fear death. It explains the conduct of the suicide bomber.

The crisis in Afghanistan has worsened in the absence of a credible strategy. Eight years after the U.S.-led invasion of 2001, the futility of counterinsurgency resulting in the loss of more innocent lives than those of "terrorists" is plain to see. To succeed, a strategy must be not about killing, but about rebuilding. It should attract support rather than cause alienation. Its foundations must be based on a thorough understanding of the cultures and sensitivities of others and reasons of human pride.

There are choices other than McChrystal's counterinsurgency plan to guide the international efforts: to persuade Pakistan's military to relax its hold; to allow the democratic institutions and processes to develop; to fight corruption; and to encourage the rule of law. Above all, to save both Afghanistan and Pakistan from future generations of militants; and to build effective systems of education that provide modern schools instead of religious madrasahs. The United States has a responsibility to play a vital role in all this. But it may only be possible if there is an acceptance in Washington that a coercive enterprise to remake a traditional society rarely succeeds.

TONY BLAIR'S IRAQ CONFESSION

December 13, 2009

Since the launch of the Iraq Inquiry in London at the end of July 2009, covers have been coming off with increasing frequency to reveal the circumstances leading to the invasion of Iraq in 2003. And not always before the inquiry chairman, John Chilcot. The latest is the admission by Tony Blair, then British prime minister and President George W. Bush's closest ally. Blair now says that he "would still have thought it right to remove" Saddam Hussein even without weapons of mass destruction; he would have had to "use and deploy different arguments" to achieve the end.

The admission, made in a BBC program, amounts to a complete repudiation of Blair's own position held since before the invasion—that British intelligence had evidence of there being weapons of mass destruction with Saddam Hussein—that some of those weapons were "deployable within 45 minutes of an order to use them"—and that he had no doubt that the threat was "serious and current." On this assessment of the British government, published in September 2002, Blair had sought the parliament's approval, which he secured in March 2003 despite a rebellion by 139 of his own MPs. The approval was made possible due to the backing of the opposition Conservative Party for the invasion of Iraq. After the vote, two senior ministers resigned from Blair's cabinet— Leader of the House, and foreign secretary earlier, Robin Cook and, some time later, International Development Secretary Clare Short. That no WMDs could be found after the invasion of Iraq has been known for several years, supporting the view of the Swedish diplomat Hans Blix, the United Nations chief weapons inspector at the time.

The timing of Blair's admission is important. It can be explained by what recent witnesses have told the Iraq Inquiry and because Blair himself is due to go before the panel in the new year. John Scarlett, former chairman of the Joint Intelligence Committee and in charge of the British intelligence assessment, made clear that the Foreword to the report was "something which was the prime minister's and it was going out under his signature." Scarlett acknowledged that the 45-minute claim was about battlefield munitions rather than long-range missiles—a distinction lost in translation. But he said that greater emphasis had been placed on the 45-minute claim in the Prime Minister's Foreword, which was "overtly political."

Suma Chakrabarti, ex-permanent secretary at the department of international development, said that evidence of the situation in Iraq before the invasion was "scanty." David Manning, former foreign policy adviser to prime minister Blair, had this to say: "George W. Bush raised the issue of Iraq with Tony Blair just three days after the 9/11 attacks, telling him during a phone conversation that Saddam Hussein may have links with al Qaeda." And Christopher Meyer, British ambassador to Washington (1997–2003): "Tony Blair's view on regime change 'tightened' after a private meeting with President Bush [in April 2002] … no officials were present at the Bush family ranch talks [in Texas], but the next day Mr Blair mentioned regime change for the first time … officials were left 'scrambling' for evidence of WMD as U.S. troops prepared for invasion."

Here is a summary of an article headlined "Lord Goldsmith warned Tony Blair over legality of the Iraq war" in The Times of London on November 30, 2009: Goldsmith, then attorney general, sent a previously undisclosed letter [in July 2002] to Blair that a war could not be justified purely on the grounds of regime change and that an invasion on the grounds of self-defense or to prevent humanitarian disaster did not apply. Blair was reported to have concealed the advice from his cabinet, fearing it would spark an anti-war revolt. Goldsmith later reaffirmed that any action had to be "proportionate" and that "regime change" could not be the objective of military action. Goldsmith was then summoned to the Prime Minister's Office and pressured, said the Times, into issuing a public statement on March 17, 2003—three days before the start of the war—that an invasion would be legal. His warning letter is said to have been submitted to the inquiry.

Blair's admission has caused a political storm. Hans Blix said that Tony Blair used WMD as a "convenient justification" for war; a Conservative

MP and member of the British Parliament's Intelligence and Security Committee, Richard Ottoway, called Blair's comments a "cynical ploy to soften up public opinion" before his appearance at the Iraq Inquiry. Former leader of Britain's Liberal Democratic Party and a distinguished barrister, Menzies Campbell, said: "I have no doubt whatsoever that if Mr Blair had told his cabinet what he is now saying, he'd have found it very difficult to keep all of them ... But the one place he would have undoubtedly failed would have been in the House of Commons."

Carol Turner of the Stop the War Coalition described it as "extraordinary" that Blair had admitted he was prepared to tailor his arguments to fit the circumstances. And Reg Keys, the father of a British soldier killed in Iraq, said he was "absolutely flabbergasted."

THE OBAMA-MCCHRYSTAL SHOWDOWN

June 23, 2010

The fate of the top United States military commander and the chief architect of American policy in Afghanistan, General Stanley McChrystal, is in the balance. General McChrystal has been summoned to explain to President Obama comments made by him and his aides to the Rolling Stone magazine. McChrystal's remarks this time have gone beyond anything the rebellious general has said in public before, rocking America's political and military establishments. Despite a prompt and profuse apology for displaying what General McChrystal admitted was poor judgment and a lack of integrity, considerable uncertainty hangs over his future.

In the article, one of McChrystal's aides was quoted as saying that the general was disappointed at his first meeting with an "unprepared" Obama, his commander-in-chief. The aide continued, "Obama clearly didn't know anything about him, who he was. Here's the guy who's going to run his ****ing war, but he didn't seem very engaged. The boss was pretty disappointed."

As part of McChrystal's strategy for "winning" the Afghan war, President Obama agreed last year to deploy more than 30,000 additional troops in the country. But he set a deadline of July 2011 for beginning a withdrawal of combat troops from Afghanistan—a political necessity before of the 2012 presidential and congressional elections. McChrystal's strategy team regards the deadline as "arbitrary." McChrystal says in the article that he felt "betrayed" by his former boss, retired General Karl Eikenberry, the current U.S. ambassador in Afghanistan. An Obama loyalist, Eikenberry was appointed to the job soon after his retirement from the military. He provided a counter to McChrystal, a hawkish warrior for whom political solutions come way behind overwhelming military power.

General McChrystal shows contempt for President Obama's special envoy for Afghanistan and Pakistan, Richard Holbrooke. An email from Holbrooke prompts McChrystal to respond, "Oh not another email from Holbrooke." The general says he doesn't even want to open it. "The boss [General McChrystal] says he [Holbrooke] is like a wounded animal. Holbrooke keeps hearing rumors that he's going to get fired, so that makes him dangerous." Then McChrystal's staff mocks Vice President Joe Biden, seen as heading the list of people against the general. And President Obama's national security advisor Jim Jones is described as a clown "stuck in 1985."

Two members of the Obama administration regarded as supporters in the McChrystal camp are Defense Secretary Robert Gates, who was retained from the Bush administration, and Secretary of State Hillary Clinton, Obama's main opponent for the Democratic nomination before the 2008 presidential election. Eighteen months after inauguration, this latest McChrystal episode illustrates something that is at the root of problems within the Obama administration. His decision to form what in effect is a coalition administration may have been well intentioned. He wanted to see potential opponents inside the tent, rather than outside. He thought he would hear differing points of view, then decide in his capacity as the nation's commander-in-chief. And everybody will obey, because the U.S. president can overrule his entire cabinet where decision-making by majority vote does not happen. It was to be his way of achieving consensus and smooth running of the administration after eight years of the Bush presidency.

The experience of the last 18 months has shown the opposite. President Obama inherited a toxic domestic and foreign-policy legacy from his predecessor. Obama's coalition of strong and ambitious personalities, of differing interests and hardnosed views, requires extraordinarily strong leadership at the top to prevail over the rest. Outside, there is America's powerful military-industrial complex, traditionally close to Republican thinking. There is the Tea Party movement, a leaderless and raucous loose network of extreme rightwing spoilers, otherwise representing a dynamic similar to the movement of moderate and progressive Americans that catapulted Obama to the White House. And a growing body of disenchanted supporters that could be as damaging to the Obama presidency as it was helpful before November 2008.

In foreign policy, a defiant Israel bent upon thwarting Obama's Middle East hopes. Iran and Turkey, largely a problem of America's own making. And the drone attacks on the Afghanistan-Pakistan front that kill many more civilians than militants. Such behavior of the U.S. military violates international law, highlights double standards and creates the impression that the commander-in-chief of the world's most powerful nation is not in control of his military.

[Subsequent to the showdown with President Obama, General Stanley McChrystal was relieved of the command in Afghanistan and retired from the army.]

THE SIGNIFICANCE OF THE AFGHAN
WAR DIARY

August 4, 2010

The Afghanistan War Diary, released by WikiLeaks, has exposed as never before a culture of lies, deceit, violence and manipulation of information in the United States-led war in that country. The volume, more than 90,000 secret records of actions taken by the American military from January 2004 to December 2009, and the depth of the culture they depict, are staggering. Their significance is immense and their release is of interest to me not least because in my book, Overcoming the Bush Legacy in Iraq and Afghanistan, published earlier this year, I have systematically identified and analyzed the Bush administration's naïve calculations, strategic and operational blunders, disregard for history and other cultures, even downright prejudices that have brought so much harm to so many. The Afghan War Diary makes a major contribution to that debate.

In historical terms, the significance of these documents is comparable to that of the Mitrokhin files uncovered nearly two decades ago. The defection of the KGB archivist Vasili Mitrokhin, with detailed notes of thousands of top secret files to Britain after the Soviet state collapsed, has long been celebrated in the West as an intelligence coup. But Mitrokhin defected after the Soviet Union had disintegrated. The Afghan Diary has been published when the West is still fighting the war in Afghanistan. Although it was already looking unlikely that the U.S.-led occupation forces would secure their adversary's surrender in Afghanistan's mountains, the publication of these documents makes it probable that the impact on public opinion will be a turning-point in the current war.

The Mitrokhin archive was an account of Soviet military-intelligence activities and culture of lies, deception and violence in great detail. The trail went deep inside Afghanistan in the decisive phase of the Cold War in the 1980s. In another book, Breeding Ground: Afghanistan and the Origins of Islamist Terrorism, I have discussed the KGB's infiltration into Afghan society in the 1960s and 1970s, as well as the Soviet security service's role before and after the December 1979 Soviet invasion of Afghanistan, based on Mitrokhin's account.

With the United States left as the only, but now increasingly tired, superpower, the Afghan Diary does something similar. It tells the story of the American military and the Central Intelligence Agency, their activities and culture during the Afghan war in the early twenty-first century. The Obama White House was quick to denounce the release of the war logs by WikiLeaks and shared with the New York Times, the Guardian and Der Spiegel. The administration called it "irresponsible" and an act that placed "troops in danger." The founder of WikiLeaks, Julian Assange, responded by saying the files showed that "thousands of war crimes" might have been committed in Afghanistan. And he promised to reveal more.

Official reaction in Washington and friendly capitals has been all over the place. President Obama's spokesman, Robert Gibbs, dismissed the leak as making no new revelations, but Washington's furious reaction against Pakistan's spy agency Inter-Services Intelligence Directorate for keeping close ties with the Afghan Taliban made it look as though the Obama administration had learned of the relationship for the first time. When asked what had changed after the disclosures, the British foreign secretary William Hague's response was "nothing." Even some seasoned journalists like the BBC's Frank Gardner said that there were "few great surprises" to those following the "twists and turns of the Afghan conflict." Some events had previously been reported in the press and keen followers of news might have suspected that other similar occurrences had taken place. What is striking here is the scale of recorded information and the pattern it points to. The Pentagon launched an immediate inquiry to find out who leaked the documents. Obviously, they came from someone within the Department of Defense.

Again, there are parallels between this and the Mitrokhin affair. The war in Afghanistan has become expensive and unpopular in the United States and elsewhere as it has progressed since the U.S.-led invasion in October 2001. Like Mitrokhin, the leaker inside the Pentagon, almost certainly a loner, must have had ready access to a huge mass of documents, probably an insider occupying a key position. The individual must have been so disillusioned with American policy as to be willing to take great personal risk in collecting and forwarding the files in electronic format to WikiLeaks.

What does the Afghanistan War Diary tell us? To what extent was the information therein already known? And what is its significance?

I said at the outset that the leaks uncover a culture of lies, deception, wanton violence and media manipulation through manufactured or wrong information. The existence of a hitherto undisclosed death squad named "Task Force 373" would go some way toward explaining that culture. TF 373, a special forces "black" unit created to hunt down targets for assassination or detention without trial, has a list of 2,000 senior Taliban and al Qaeda figures. The documents reveal that, in many cases, the black squad simply killed suspected "militants" without attempting to capture them. Its members also killed civilian men, women and children, even Afghan police officers who came in their way.

A deeply frightening pattern of extrajudicial killings of innocent civilians emerges. In May 2008, the United Nations special rapporteur Philip Alston went to Afghanistan to investigate reports of gratuitous violence against innocent civilians and "suspected militants" against whom nothing had been proven. Alston warned that foreign forces in Afghanistan were neither transparent nor accountable. Afghans who attempted to find out who killed their loved ones "often came away empty handed, frustrated and bitter." Fifty-two civilian deaths were recently reported with graphic pictures on international television of the scene of destruction and villagers digging graves for their loved ones. Local residents of Rigi village in Sangin district gave accounts of how missiles were fired from air, resulting in the carnage. The Afghan president Hamid Karzai bitterly complained. A terse NATO statement said "there was no evidence of casualties beyond insurgents," and that a joint NATO-Afghan government investigation was going on.

I describe acts of indiscriminate killing by U.S.-led forces from the beginning of the war on Afghanistan in October 2001 in Overcoming the Bush Legacy. Although the WikiLeaks War Diary starts more than two years later in January 2004, the origins of the culture of violence can be traced back to the late 1970s. Then a small group of pro-Soviet Afghan nationalists seized power in Kabul. President Jimmy Carter began a secret program of aid to Mujahideen groups fighting the pro-Moscow government. As the conflict escalated from a low-level guerrilla campaign, Soviet leader Leonid Brezhnev ordered a military invasion of Afghanistan in December 1979. I discuss in Breeding Ground how President Carter's national security advisor Zbigniew Brzezinski came out with the idea to lure the Soviets into Afghanistan, to give them "their Vietnam." The Soviet Union lost and disintegrated. But the war in Afghanistan never ceased. In the first decade of the twenty-first century, decisions taken by George W. Bush and Barack Obama have been like pouring oil on the fire. The Guardian newspaper said on July 25, 2010:

"Now, for the first time, the leaked war logs reveal details of deadly missions by TF 373 and other units hunting down Jpel targets that were previously hidden behind a screen of misinformation. They raise fundamental questions about the legality of the killings and of the long-term imprisonment without trial, and also pragmatically about the impact of a tactic which is inherently likely to kill, injure and alienate the innocent bystanders whose support the coalition craves."

The Afghanistan War Diary is littered with accounts of civilian casualties, ranging from shootings of innocent people to air attacks resulting in massive loss of life. American and allied commanders often deny these incidents, describing them either as Taliban propaganda or claiming that the dead were Taliban insurgents. One incident would illustrate this. In September 2009, there was a major scandal in the northern Kunduz province, where a German commander ordered the bombing of a crowd looting two hijacked fuel tankers. The immediate log note circulated to NATO allies recorded him authorizing the attack by an American F-15 jet "after ensuring that no civilians were in the vicinity." The "battle damage assessment" confirmed, it claimed, that 56 purely "enemy insurgents" had died. Media reports forced an official inquiry, which concluded that there had been "between thirty and seventy civilian deaths."

The War Diary goes on to record several instances of the insurgents firing on American aircraft that were suppressed from the public records. In May 2007, a Chinook helicopter was hit by a missile in Helmand, killing everyone on board. The United States claimed that the helicopter was struck by "lucky shot from a rocket propelled grenade" with no heat-seeking device. A month before that incident, a British Chinook helicopter crew had reported that a missile passed the aircraft before exploding just 50 feet from it. And in July 2007, the crew of a C-130 transport plane reported that a rocket flew past as they refueled at 11,000 feet. Despite official denials, there is evidence that the risk is taken seriously. Military aircraft leaving flares to distract enemy missiles are regularly seen in the sky.

It is worth recalling President Reagan's decision to supply heat-seeking Stinger missiles to anti-Soviet fighters in Afghanistan in 1986. Reagan's move turned the tide against the Soviet occupation forces. Britain supplied less sophisticated, but still lethal, Blowpipe missiles to the Afghan resistance. The decision by President Reagan and his CIA director William Casey, both avowed anti-Communists, to supply the hi-tech Stinger missiles is discussed at length in my book Breeding Ground. There had been a fierce debate in the CIA and the Defense Department for many months before their delivery to the anti-Soviet Afghan forces via Pakistan. Some in the Reagan administration strongly opposed the move, arguing that the weapon was too advanced to pass on to unreliable forces. But I explain in Breeding Ground that Reagan and Casey were determined to make any sacrifice and pay any price to ensure that the Soviet Union was defeated. They appeared to have no regard for future consequences.

As I write this article, reports are coming in of another German reconnaissance plane being lost in Kunduz province, a Taliban stronghold in the north where insurgent activity has been spreading. It will be the fourth German aircraft to have been lost in Afghanistan this year. In my book Breeding Ground I make the point that the Stinger anti-aircraft missile had highly advanced heat-seeking missile technology in the 1980s. Its deployment in Afghanistan via Pakistan's spy agency ISI came with the obvious risk that the technology could one day be used against the United States and allies. Now the Afghanistan War Diary raises the haunting question: Have the Taliban, and by implication Pakistani intelligence, got that technology" If so, the consequences for the West and for Pakistan's traditional adversary India are ominous.

That there continues to be a close relationship between Pakistan's ISI and the Afghan Taliban is neither new, nor surprising. Afghanistan is a frail neighboring state bordering on Pakistan. Pakistan's interest in Afghanistan is a historical fact of the region's politics. It is surprising that the Bush administration was naïve enough to forge an anti-Taliban alliance with Pakistan's military ruler General Pervez Musharraf within hours of the September 11, 2001 attacks. And President Obama continues to hope that the present military-civilian ruling establishment will deliver despite South Asia's geopolitics pointing in the opposite direction.

THE LONELINESS OF BARACK OBAMA

November 9, 2010

The moment when President Obama emerged at the White House to speak to the press on November 4, less than twenty-four hours after the Democratic Party's midterm drubbing, provided the most telling picture. There was the president of the world's most powerful country walking alone to the podium, admitting defeat just two years after an historic triumph so complete that it was hailed as a revolutionary event. As he stood uncomfortably to express contrition and promise that lessons would be learned, there was nobody from his administration standing with him to show support after a defeat as decisive as the victory was magnificent over the discredited Republican Party in 2008.

Vice President Joe Biden had appeared at election rallies as the president tried to enthuse voters in the final days of campaigning. However, the vice president was nowhere to be seen when Obama walked to the podium to face the world. Neither was the Secretary of State Hillary Clinton. One of the oddities of this campaign, dominated by the economy, was the absence of debate on America's foreign wars and their consequences, economic or otherwise. Talking to Amy Goodman on Democracy Now!, a vocal critic on America's political left, Michael Moore, gave a penetrating explanation. The liberal political class had gone along with, even surrendered to, many of the neoconservative war policies in the last decade. Now the same liberal class lives with guilt, and does not want to talk about war because it has been an accomplice.

The heroin of the American neoliberals, Hillary Clinton, has long engaged in warmongering. For her, it would not make sense to appear with Obama in a moment of abject failure. It is safe to assume that her presidential ambition still flickers. In October, Obama's chief of staff, Rahm Emanuel, had left the administration, saying he wanted to pursue his ambition to become mayor of Chicago. His term as Obama's chief henchman has been an unmitigated disaster. A Jewish American with longstanding ties with Israel, Emanuel's appointment after Obama's election was greeted with dismay. Emanuel's obsession with the art of wheeling-dealing was well known. His mastery of colorful and abusive language was no secret in Washington. His fascination with CIA drone attacks and phone calls to the agency's director to find out "Who did we get today?" has been written about.

The Palestinians, the Iranians and others in the Middle East were not going to have faith in an Obama administration with someone like Emanuel playing a pivotal role. The collapse of Obama's dream of resolving the Israel-Palestinian conflict, and peace with the Muslim world, is partly Emanuel's legacy. With Emanuel gone, neither the interim chief of staff Pete Rouse nor his deputies were by the president's side when he spoke to the press following the midterm debacle. Not a single Democratic member of the old or new House, or the Senate, was to be seen with him, even a Senator not up for reelection; and not a member of the Democratic National Committee, which has its headquarters in Washington, D.C.

Obama's national security adviser, retired Marine Corp general James Jones, had also left in October. As war had not been part of the national debate in the midterm campaign, the incoming Security Advisor Thomas Donilon or Defense Secretary Robert Gates were not expected to be visible at the postelection news conference. In any case, Gates continues to threaten to leave the administration from time to time. More significant was the non-visibility of any member of President Obama's economic team. In September, as the economy looked certain to be the dominant campaign issue and polling day drew closer, two of his leading advisers, Lawrence Summers and Christina Romer, had announced that they were leaving. On the day after the midterm debacle, President Obama stood all by himself to face questions about his handling of the economy.

After nearly an hour explaining the defeat, empathizing with the American people's difficulties and offering to cooperate with the unbending and unbendable Republicans and tea partiers in the new Congress, Obama's lone walk back into the Oval Office was symbolic of the wreckage lying around a president once known for his audacity of hope. America's political establishment remains engaged in civil war. The country is deeply unhappy and polarized. And the leader chosen by the majority of Americans, no less because of overwhelming support from liberals and progressives, is ready to walk away from his troops toward the confronting army, alone, to compromise.

AMERICA, IRAN AND AN INTERVENTIONIST SECRETARY OF STATE

October 16, 2011

The war is not over yet in Libya after the overthrow of Muammar Gaddafi and the Obama administration has turned its attention to Iran. Attorney General Eric Holder's announcement of a "plot" to assassinate the Saudi ambassador in the United States, and warnings of dire consequences for Iran, mark a new escalation between the two countries. The Obama administration says the offender behind the "plot" is an Iranian-American used-car salesman based in Texas, Mansour Arbabsiar, who believed he was hiring assassins from a Mexican drug cartel for a meager one and a half million dollars. It was a trap set up by federal agents. Not for the first time, it seems, the American law enforcement agencies are responsible for planting ideas into the mind of someone naïve and ordinary and making an arrest as soon as the individual looks interested.

The evidence has to be tested in courts. Reports say the man in custody will plead "not guilty," but the Obama administration has already found him guilty. Further, according to the Obama administration, the trail points all the way to the Iranian regime. That the government in Tehran would use an American citizen of Iranian descent to hatch a scheme with a Mexican drug cartel to kill the Saudi ambassador to the United States, involving less than two million dollars, looks bizarre. Why the Saudi ambassador and not a bigger target? For a relatively small sum? Why would the authorities in Tehran take such a risk? What purpose would be served? Honest answers to these and other perplexing questions are difficult to come by. Juan Cole, Middle East scholar at the University of Michigan, raises even more questions and concludes why it could not be the work of the Iranian government. Tehran rejects Washington's accusations.

There will be those who will see the latest developments as part of a consistent pattern of U.S. foreign policy conduct in the Middle East, especially with regard to Iran. The motive—to teach Iran a lesson in any way possible. Like the accusations against Muammar Gaddafi that he was employing mass rape of women as a weapon against opponents, to justify NATO's war in Libya. Human rights organizations like Amnesty plainly contradicted the U.S. secretary of state, Hillary Clinton, and the prosecutor of the International Criminal Court, Luis Moreno-Ocampo, who made the fantastic claim that "we have information that there was a policy to rape in Libya those who were against the government. Apparently he [Colonel Gaddafi] used it to punish people."

Now, as doubts increase over the "plot," but the campaign against Iran is pushed by Washington regardless, expressions of incredulity abound. Veterans Today, American servicemen's magazine, has an article titled "Mr. President, We Believe Holder Lied on Iran Terror." Senior editor Gordon Duff commented, "Within 24 hours of the announcement of a new Iranian plot, the truth started leaking out. That leak is now a flood. The FBI made up the whole thing, invented it and you and they aren't going to get away with it. Why something this outrageous, this incompetent?"

There seems to be no limit to which Hillary Clinton's war of vengeance will go. It is worth noting her unrestrained outburst about Iran during the final phase of her unsuccessful bid for the Democratic Party's nomination in the 2008 presidential election. She said that as president she would "totally obliterate" Iran if it foolishly considered attacking Israel— a scenario not very likely. Contrary to what some in Washington's corridors of power think, the Iranians are more sensible than they are given credit for. At the time, Hillary Clinton's opponent, Barack Obama, dismissed her outburst as "sabre rattling."

The Obama administration's character today is vastly different from Obama the candidate's. Hillary Clinton, ex-New York senator and a committed supporter of Israel, is his secretary of state. I believe she is the most powerful figure to have arrived at the top in the State Department since Henry Kissinger during the Nixon presidency more than 35 years ago. Even then, Nixon was a formidable liberal figure in international politics. An architect of détente, his foreign policy goals were radically different from Washington's objectives in the twenty-first century.

Hillary Clinton is arguably the most interventionist secretary of state in the past half century. While Obama struggles at home with an increasingly belligerent Congress, Hillary Clinton has, in effect, seized control of U.S. foreign policy, which she conducts with far less diplomacy than military threats. Like the Bush-Cheney administration, we are witnessing an Obama-Clinton presidency brazenly engaging in targeted killings in any country it wishes and, at the same time, accuses another country of plotting an assassination in Washington. A Democratic administration has embraced the neoconservative Project for the New American Century, and its aggressiveness and folly compete with each other.

CHAPTER THREE:

HUMILIATION AND RESISTANCE

OBAMA'S AFGHAN SURGE

December 28, 2008

Nearly 30 years after the Cold War exploded into full-scale conflict in Afghanistan, the incoming president, Barack Obama, is about to embark on yet another stage in America's involvement in that country. In short hand, it is described as Obama's "Afghan surge." If a recent report in the New York Times is anything to go by, the "Afghan surge" would be remarkably similar to the "surge" of 2007 in Iraq under President George W. Bush.

The "Iraqi surge" was an attempt to subdue the rapidly escalating cycle of violence in the capital, Baghdad, and Anbar Province covering much of western Iraq. The buildup involved the deployment of 30,000 extra U.S. troops as part of "The New Way Forward" announced by Bush in January 2007. Barely six weeks before, the Washington Post had disclosed a U.S. intelligence report admitting that "the social and political situation has deteriorated to a point" that American and Iraqi troops "are no longer capable of militarily defeating the insurgency" in Anbar. From village to provincial levels, nearly all government institutions had collapsed. Summarizing the assessment, one American military officer said, "We have been defeated politically—and that's where wars are won and lost."

The situation in much of Afghanistan and Pakistan is grim, and reaches beyond the borders of Pakistan. Militants launch audacious attacks from their bases on both sides of the Afghan-Pakistan frontier. Events in recent months have demonstrated that Kabul, Islamabad, Delhi or Mumbai—no major city in the region is safe. Violence in the countryside in Afghanistan and Pakistan goes on largely unnoticed, unless it involves foreign forces.

I referred to similarities between the "Iraqi surge" and the "Afghan surge" earlier. American and British media report that as many as 30,000 extra troops are to be deployed on the Afghan front by summer 2009.

According to the New York Times, preparations are underway "to arm local militias to help in the fight against a resurgent Taleban" in Afghanistan. The government of Pakistan is unlikely to give its official consent to the arming of militias inside its territory. There are several reasons. Contrary to popular belief in the West, the Taliban are not a homogeneous group, but a loose network bound by a certain interpretation of Islam. The Taliban of Pakistan are firmly embedded in Pakistani society, where the culture of weapons is all pervasive.

Relations between Islamabad and Washington, and Islamabad and Delhi, have suffered a sharp deterioration. The perception is strong in the ruling establishment of Pakistan that America has switched its support to India. Three main factors are responsible for this change in U.S. policy: Pakistan's failure to contain the militant groups in its territory, China's emergence as a major power and America's growing economic and military ties with India.

The shift in American policy towards India is likely to continue during the Obama presidency. It means a break in Washington's strategic alliance with Islamabad going back to the 1950s as part of the policy of containment of the Soviet Union. One of America's long-term aims now is to counter the growing power of China. But the military-political establishment of Pakistan will see it as encirclement of the country while the occupation forces remain in Afghanistan to the west and U.S. ties grow with India to the east. There is also a perception in Pakistan that the country does rather better under military dictators as an ally of the United States than under a fledgling democracy.

What more does the "Afghan surge" indicate beyond introducing as many as 30,000 more troops and recruiting militias to fight the Taliban? In the case of Iraq, most of the extra U.S. soldiers were deployed in Baghdad with the stated aim of improving security in the capital. The tour of duty of several thousand troops already in Baghdad was extended. Many were deployed in Anbar Province, which had suffered some of the worst violence. A report by the Senlis Council think-tank in November 2007 estimated that more than half of Afghanistan had fallen back under Taliban control.

If anything, the situation worsened in 2008. Anti-government forces, enriched by the illicit profits from Afghanistan's poppy harvest, set up de facto administration in large areas of the Pashtun belt in the south and the east. Insurgents penetrated the security ring around the capital, Kabul. Attacks on government and foreign targets were launched with increasing frequency. The most audacious of them was on the Indian embassy in July 2008.

As part of the "Afghan surge" many of the additional U.S. troops are likely to be deployed around the capital, Kabul, as they were in Baghdad in 2007. The need to protect the American and allied embassies, diplomats, Afghan ministries and officials is paramount. Offices of many non-governmental organizations are located in Kabul, and it is vital to project Kabul's image as a secure and stable seat of government—image that has suffered as the situation has steadily worsened. The International (Green) Zone in Baghdad would serve as the model where occupation forces and Iraqi government are concentrated. Surrounded by blast-proof walls, barbed wire-fences and a few checkpoints to control entry, it is in effect a mini-city inside the Iraqi capital. In contrast, Kabul is a sprawling, chaotic town and fortification of a similar kind would be more difficult.

The other side of Obama's "Afghan surge" is to recruit local militias to fight the Taliban. As the New York Times says, this has raised fears that "the new armed groups could push the country into a deeper bloodletting." Shi'a and other minorities are already concerned over the prospect of new Sunni militias roaming parts of Afghanistan, supposedly to fight the Taliban. Once again, the plan originates from Iraq. American officials say that their decision to recruit 100,000 Sunni tribesmen, many ex-rebel fighters, under the umbrella of Awakening Councils was responsible for the "steep reduction" in violence. The logic is that what worked in one country would also work in the other.

In truth, it is too early to claim success in Iraq. American casualties have declined after the handover of security to the Iraqis, but acts of bombing, shooting, abduction and extortion continue almost every day. Under American pressure, the Shi'a-dominated government in Baghdad took over the responsibility of paying salaries to the Awakening Council militias. However, the government remains opposed to assimilating more than a small proportion of them into the regular armed forces. The Shi'a majority of Iraq, together with Iran, will view the Sunni militias as Saudi Arabia's proxy. The militiamen see an uncertain future for themselves as the occupation forces draw down and Obama turns his attention to Afghanistan.

We have seen it all before. Following the 1978 Communist coup by a group of army officers in Afghanistan, President Jimmy Carter ordered secret aid to the Mujahideen in that country. Encouraged by the American CIA and its close ally, Pakistan, Mujahideen guerrillas increased pressure on the Communist regime. The Soviet leadership panicked and invaded Afghanistan to maintain control of a country it regarded as within its sphere of influence. From 1981, President Ronald Reagan, Carter's successor, armed and financed more than 80,000 guerrillas to fight America's proxy war against the Soviet Union.

For almost two decades, the "official version" of history promoted by Washington had suggested that America's military aid to the Mujahideen came after the Soviet invasion of a poor, helpless country. The truth was rather more complex. In 1996, the CIA's former director, Robert Gates, revealed that the Carter administration had begun to look at ways of providing covert assistance to the anti-Communist forces soon after the 1978 coup in Afghanistan. And in July 1979, nearly six months before the Soviets invaded, Carter issued a directive authorizing secret aid to the Mujahideen.

Zbigniew Brzezinski, Carter's national security advisor, spoke in public about the matter for the first time in 1998. He confirmed that Carter did issue the order that started the secret aid program for the Mujahideen. Brzezinski also revealed that he told Carter the American action was "going to induce a Soviet military intervention" in Afghanistan. Brzezinski described it as "an excellent idea," because it had the effect of drawing the Soviet Union into the "Afghan trap." On the day the Soviets invaded Afghanistan, Brzezinski said, he wrote to the president that the United States now had "the opportunity to give the USSR its Vietnam War."

In 1989, the Soviet occupation forces retreated from Afghanistan, just as the United States had done from Vietnam in 1975. The Soviet Union paid the ultimate price, its own demise, barely three years later. The Communist regime in Afghanistan collapsed a few months after the Soviet state had disintegrated, like the fall of America's client regime in South Vietnam more than 15 years before. The Mujahideen march into

Kabul was greeted with delight in Washington, and the United States moved on to new priorities. They were to manage the disintegration of the Soviet state and its nuclear arsenal, to oversee the expansion of the free-market system abroad and to help the American economy.

Afghan factions had been supplied with weapons, money and copies of the Qur'an by President Reagan's CIA chief, William Casey, in the 1980s. In the ruins of war, they were left to fight it out in the 1990s. The civil war gave rise to the Taliban and Afghanistan became a sanctuary for al Qaeda. Now, after eight years of failed war in Afghanistan under the Bush presidency, comes the latest twist. President Obama's "Afghan surge" will not only involve extra American troops to defend Kabul and other strategic points, it will include the hiring and arming of pro-U.S. local militias to fight the Taliban in the countryside. And according to a recent report in the Washington Post, the CIA has begun to supply the sex-enhancing drug, Viagra, to Afghan chiefs to gain information about Taliban activities.

In the Cold War, the CIA handed out money, weapons and copies of the Qur'an to Islamic groups to fight against Soviet communism. Two decades later, the agency has added Viagra to its list of temptations to lure Afghans in the U.S. war against the Taliban and al Qaeda.

KABUL SUICIDE BOMBER TARGETS NATO TROOPS

May 18, 2010

A suicide car bomb attack targeting NATO troops has killed about 20 people near parliament in the capital Kabul. More than 50 others were wounded. An army doctor said it was the worst bombing in the city for more than a year. The Taliban immediately claimed responsibility, saying they had targeted "invading NATO forces." The insurgents said they used a van loaded with 750 kilos of explosives. The attack came in the midst of U.S.-led military operations in Helmand Province and in the Taliban stronghold, Kandahar. Success in these operations would be essential for President Obama's intended withdrawal of U.S. combat troops to begin in July 2011.

In a comment, the BBC security correspondent Nick Childs said, "The Western alliance is making no bones about the fact that it is trying to wrest the military initiative in Afghanistan from the insurgents. So, in the battle for perceptions and hearts and minds, this will be a serious blow, with the high loss of life both of NATO troops and local civilians." A spokesman for the international peacekeeping force confirmed that six of its soldiers had been killed. Apart from the five U.S. soldiers, one Canadian was believed to have died. However, most of the casualties were civilians, as is the case in most attacks by combatants.

In another attack inside Pakistan, at least 12 people were killed by a bomb near a police vehicle in the northwestern Pakistani town of Dera Ismail Khan. According to officials, the device was planted on a bicycle and targeted the deputy police superintendent, who was killed along with his guard and driver. There have been a number of U.S. drone attacks inside Pakistan since the attempted bomb attack in New York in early May. An American citizen of Pakistani origin, Faisal Shahzad, is in custody as the main suspect and is being interrogated. And the Secretary of State Hillary Clinton has warned of serious consequences for Pakistan if security threats appeared to originate from there. As President

Obama's deadline of July 2011 for a military drawdown approaches, violence on both sides is likely to increase.

AFGHANISTAN, THE END GAME?

June 25, 2011

When the president of the United States makes a long-awaited statement about matters of war and peace, it is an important moment. President Barack Obama's announcement on June 22 that he plans to bring 33,000 American troops home from Afghanistan in the next 15 months is another milestone in a long war that is reminiscent of the 1980s, and the Soviet experience in that country at great cost. In February 1986, barely a year after coming to power, the Soviet leader Mikhail Gorbachev described Afghanistan as a "bleeding wound"—a legacy of the previous Kremlin leadership that took the fateful decision to invade that country in December 1979. In Obama's words, "We have learned anew the profound cost of war." Nearly 4,500 Americans have paid with their lives in Iraq, some 1,500 in Afghanistan, and a trillion dollars have been spent on war at a time of rising debt and hard economic times.

It is beyond doubt that policymakers of the first Bush administration (2001–2005), full of hubris and fascination with the "long war," over-stretched the United States. Those errors and the costs they incurred have sapped the will and resources of America and its allies. The full-blown crisis that struck the United States economy, with dire consequences for others, had much to do with America's long war, even though banks can hardly escape their share of responsibility for the economic system's failure. According to the defense and intelligence consultancy STRATFOR, supplying a single gallon of petrol in Afghanistan costs an average of 400 dollars to the U.S. military and sustaining one soldier around a million dollars. With less than 18 months to go before the November 2012 election, Obama's primary concern must be the American economy, which shows little sign of improvement.

Obama's announcement is not without significance, but nor should its significance be exaggerated. His record on the Guantanamo Bay detention camp, trial by military tribunals, torture and extrajudicial killings,

drone attacks and other matters of civil liberties inside and outside the
United States is mixed. In light of that record, his mind could change
anytime between now and November 2012. For those who admired
and supported the old-style Soviet regime, Mikhail Gorbachev is an
anathema, because his name will forever be associated with the demise
of the Soviet state. Gorbachev's supporters inside the ex-Soviet Union
cannot be more than a tiny number. Obama, the leader of the other
colossus, still fights for his political career and eventual legacy. However, it has become clear by now that President Obama's actions are not
determined by high principles and consistency. Gorbachev, the Soviet
leader, staked everything to make the Soviet Union a liberal, open and
reformed society.

President Obama's announcement of his drawdown plan between
now and summer 2012 is driven by pressing economic needs and political expediency. The total of U.S. and NATO troops in Afghanistan
was around 140,000 strong at the beginning of June 2011. Even if the
withdrawal was completed as planned, the remaining American forces
would be around 68,000, about the same as before Obama's "surge," and
foreign troops in excess of 100,000 strong. His reelection campaign
has just got underway. A formidable coalition has emerged in the U.S.
Congress advocating a speedy withdrawal from Afghanistan, encouraged
by opinion polls showing strong support to bring the war to an end.

However, these forces are confronted by the ever powerful military-
industrial complex and the Pentagon hierarchy that feel threatened by
significant reductions in what they do. Their opposition to Obama's
plan is hardly surprising, nor is it likely that the pressure on the president would cease during this timetable and beyond. The supreme irony
with Obama's surge is that 2010 was still the bloodiest year on the
Afghanistan-Pakistan front, and the level of violence shows no sign of
abating. A decade of war and the costs thereof seem to have caused a
breach between America's military lobby and at least some of the political establishment. The killing of Osama bin Laden by U.S. special forces
has strengthened President Obama's "war credentials." So he can now
talk about peace. Only a few days ago, President Karzai of Afghanistan
and the U.S. Defense Secretary Robert Gates, probably for different
reasons, spoke of talks with the Taliban.

What Washington says London often repeats. Consistent with that pattern, the British Foreign Secretary William Hague proclaimed that his government was also talking with the Taliban. The mainstream media in the United States, Britain and elsewhere, ever hungry for their 24-hour news operations, portrayed those statements as a "disclosure." But the talk of direct and indirect contacts with the Taliban is nothing new. The biggest problem for the United States remains persuading the Taliban to stop fighting, possibly accept a role of some sort, and let American military bases with thousands of "noncombatant" troops stay in Afghanistan. It is difficult to see that the Taliban will accept that.

AFGHANISTAN AND PALESTINE—SETBACKS AGAIN

September 26, 2011

All eyes were focused on the game of brinkmanship over the Palestinians' bid for full United Nations membership when Afghanistan's ethnic Tajik leader and ex-president Burhanuddin Rabbani was assassinated in Kabul on September 20. Rabbani's murder has to do with past rivalries, as well as the future, of Afghanistan and is significant, as is the battle for Palestinian statehood. The stakes are high in each case. What will transpire seems uncertain at this stage.

The Palestinians' bid to enhance their status in the United Nations is not necessarily doomed in the face of the United States veto, and Israel's brute military force against the Palestinian population in the occupied territories. The Palestinians' move does not alter the reality on the ground for now, but has the potential to transform international diplomacy, isolating the Obama and Netanyahu administrations. A vote in the United Nations General Assembly could then upgrade Palestine to be a "UN non-member state," putting it alongside the Vatican, Kosovo and Taiwan. It would be short of full statehood, but a significant push.

Freedom from occupation comes after a long struggle and great sacrifices. It has been the case in the past and it is certainly the case with the Palestinians. I am old enough to remember apartheid in South Africa, and how that system created a messy network of affluent white communities living off the labor of blacks of Bantustans, existing at the mercy of the Afrikaner regime. The power of anti-apartheid campaigners inside South Africa was no match compared to the power of the rulers. But the virtue of their cause gave them inner strength. Their plight transformed the world opinion slowly, but decidedly. Today, the U.S. administration brandishes its veto because Israel's military power is not enough. What is blindingly obvious to much of the rest of the world is the cruelty and injustice of the system of expanding illegal Jewish settlements and shrinking Palestinian towns and villages, separated by the wall. It stands as a monument of colonization and wrong done to Palestinians. Attempts to create a social order of this nature often fail, and the cost is often great.

For now, though, in the midst of an economic crisis, the issue of Palestine is the last thing President Obama wants to deal with, for it threatens his reelection in 2012. Obama's remarks before an audience representing 193 member-states overwhelmingly supportive of the Palestinian bid in the General Assembly marked a dark, shameful day for the United Nations and the United States. Uri Avnery, founder of the Israeli peace movement Gush Shalom and former Knesset member, reacted by saying, "Almost every statement in the passage concerning the Israeli-Palestinian issue was a lie." Avnery described Obama at his best, and at his worst. The anger on the Palestinian side was profound.

While the demand for a "two-state solution" is under the spotlight, there is another side to the debate that is even more nightmarish for Israel's hardline Jews and their friends. It is the idea of a single democratic state with Jews, Palestinians and Christians, all living as equal citizens of the same state. It may look farfetched. However, as illegal Jewish settlements continue to squeeze the Palestinian land in the West Bank and Gaza, and an independent Palestinian state becomes less and less viable, the idea of a single Israel-Palestine gains credence. The Palestinian leadership of Fatah and Hamas must be aware of the prospect. For the more diehard committed to the idea of an Islamic or Jewish state, it may be beyond contemplation. But for liberal Jews and Palestinians, and others outside, it is not such a fantastic idea.

Imagine the unthinkable. Four million Palestinians of the West Bank and Gaza with nearly eight million citizens of present-day Israel, including six million Jews, the rest Arab Israelis and others, all enjoying equal rights under the same constitution. The Israeli-Palestinian conflict has a long, destructive history behind and similarly a difficult road ahead. However, it is beginning to point to a destination, still distant, not quite certain, and unpalatable for the Israeli ruling elite and those in friendly capitals.

The assassination of Burhanuddin Rabbani in Kabul temporarily overshadowed the Palestinian debate in New York. Much has been made in the western press about the setback the assassination has delivered, because it is said that Rabbani was the chairman of the Afghan Peace Council, an appointment by President Hamid Karzai. In truth, the reasons behind Rabbani's murder have much more to do with the Cold War and Afghanistan's ethnic and political rivalries that go 50 years back—rivalries that I discuss in my book, Breeding Ground: Afghanistan and the Origins of Islamist Terrorism (Potomac, 2011).

Rabbani, an ethnic Tajik from the north, was a founder of the Islamist party, Jamiat-e-Islami, and a theology lecturer at Kabul University in the 1960s. His bitter rival was Gulbuddin Hikmatyar, a Pashtun student in the faculty of engineering, and a leading figure in the Pashtun fundamentalist group, Hizb-i-Islami, which later split. Both were violently opposed to Afghanistan's secular ruling elite. Their hatred for each other was to continue through the 1980s, when both fought the Soviet occupation forces with the CIA's help. Their rivalry grew more intense as Hikmatyar became Pakistan's favorite, receiving the largest amount of Western weaponry and money from Saudi Arabia, channeled through Pakistan's military intelligence service ISI.

When the Soviet Union withdrew in 1989 and the last Afghan Communist leader Najibullah was ousted three years later, open warfare broke out between Hikmatyar's and Rabbani's forces. Rabbani was president of Afghanistan during the years of factional war between 1992 and 1996. Then the Taliban, successors of the Mujahideen, pushed Rabbani's forces out of the capital, Kabul. Thereafter, he was president only in name until the Taliban were ousted following the September 11, 2001 attacks on America.

Gulbuddin Hikmatyar has moved closer to the Taliban, fighting the U.S.-led foreign troops in Afghanistan. Rabbani was living in a heavily guarded mansion in Kabul, supposedly assisting President Karzai in achieving reconciliation with the Taliban. But the process under Rabbani's chairmanship was a nonstarter from the beginning, and has ended in his assassination by a suicide bomber who supposedly had gone to visit him for talks.

Two days before the September 11, 2001 attacks, Rabbani's military chief Ahmad Shah Massoud was murdered by al Qaeda suicide bombers posing as journalists. The writing had been on the wall ever since for Burhanuddin Rabbani. The prospects of a controversial Tajik figure like Rabbani succeeding in negotiations with the Taliban were already remote. His assassination is like oil in the fires long raging between Afghanistan's two biggest ethnic groups.

RUTHLESSLY PURSUING MIDDLE EAST STRATEGY

November 20, 2011

Popular uprisings that began with peaceful protests in Tunisia and Algeria nearly a year ago, and spread across the Arab world, have created a new reality, not only in countries to experience political awakening, but far beyond. More worryingly for Washington, the Arab Spring has created fresh uncertainties and pressures for United States policy. With the first anniversary of those momentous events approaching, there is growing resentment among many Arabs who feel that their revolutions have been hijacked by forces not originally anticipated. Demonstrations in Egypt, Jordan, Bahrain and Kuwait in the last few days are acute symptoms of the prevailing mood in the region.

Two opposing trends are at work. The pressure from below succeeded in overthrowing the regimes in Algeria and Tunisia and President Hosni Mubarak, though not the ruling military order, in Egypt. But the pressure from above has been decisive in the overthrow and lynching of Libya's Muammar Gaddafi after NATO's intervention. It also continues to sustain Bahrain's minority Sunni ruling class, thanks to the entry of Saudi troops and Western military assistance. In Syria, Bashar al-Assad is much more resilient, despite every conceivable attempt by the United States and its Arab and European allies. I say "every conceivable attempt" because the prospect of the United Nations Security Council approving a Libya-type full-scale Western-led intervention in Syria is less likely. The Russians and the Chinese are unlikely to give their consent to such a move by America, Britain and France.

Even so, external forces look determined to decide Syria's fate. A lot depends on whether the Syrian armed forces will mostly remain loyal to the regime. Rumors of defections from the Syrian military abound, but for now the military as an institution appears to be with Assad—just about. However, with the United States determined eventually to see regime change in Syria too, the course of events there could be even more bloody. Its implications for the Middle East, starting from neighboring Lebanon, will be very serious indeed.

What began so hopefully in the Arab world a year ago has transpired into something bloody and ugly. Authoritarian regimes assisted and sustained by great powers have long dominated the region. Although the Cold War ended and the Soviet threat ceased more than two decades ago, the United States continues to pursue its grand strategy in the region with increasing vigor. The need for oil and support for Israel remain the two fundamental planks of U.S. foreign policy. The Arab Spring threatened the status quo, and with it America's interests, in the Middle East. It had to be reversed.

What we see now is a counterrevolution from above, trying to frustrate the will of the people. After Libya, the only exception is Syria. Democracy would be very welcome there, as it would be throughout the Arab world, but turmoil inspired by foreign powers is not what the region needs. The supreme irony is that both Libya and Syria, now being targeted by Washington on grounds of humanitarian intervention, had actually collaborated with the torture program during America's "war on terror." The Libyan and Syrian regimes accepted detainees rendered by the U.S. and British intelligence agencies and tortured them in their notorious prisons. As for old friends like Abdelaziz Bouteflika of Algeria, Zine El Abidine Ben Ali of Tunisia and Hosni Mubarak of Egypt, they had to be abandoned, having served their purpose and become liabilities. The tide of popular opposition to them had become unstoppable.

Political expediency demanded that they be sacrificed in the interest of Washington's alliance with the military in Egypt, Algeria and Tunisia, and the pace of change be controlled. Emboldened by Washington's understanding and encouragement, the Egyptian military has been tightening its grip in the country. A climate of fear and sorrow pervades the streets of Cairo in advance of parliamentary elections beginning on November 28. And in response to calls for limiting military assistance to Egypt, Secretary of State Hillary Clinton has reaffirmed that the United States is against "imposing any conditions."

Egypt is the biggest, most powerful country in the Arab world. Compliance of Egypt and Saudi Arabia, the leading oil exporter and most influential country in the Islamic world, is vital for Israeli security and continuing U.S. supremacy in the Middle East. Hence it is vital for the Obama administration that the rulers of Egypt and Saudi Arabia, with smaller Gulf states, remain beholden to Washington.

Double standards of international law for friends and foes is the name of the game while the United States pursues its grand strategy in the Middle East. Not learning lessons from the calamitous legacy of America's wars under the Reagan presidency in the 1980s, and more recently from George W. Bush's "war on terror," it is "Carry On Barack Obama." As we approach the next chapter of recent bloody history, it is difficult to escape a deeper sense of foreboding.

A Persian Response to Brinkmanship

December 5, 2011

Perils of brinkmanship with Iran are now on open display. As Libyans struggle after the overthrow of Muammar Gaddafi, and the rebellion against the Bashar al-Assad regime in Syria continues, the campaign of sanctions against Iran has triggered events which echo the 1980s crisis between post-revolution Iran and the West. The recent International Atomic Energy Agency report, a controversial document censoring Iran, Britain's decision to severe links with Iran's central banking system and further sanctions by France, Canada and the United States were all too much.

The Iranian parliament retaliated by downgrading relations with the United Kingdom and told the new British ambassador to leave. Soon after, angry protesters stormed two British embassy compounds in Tehran. Property was damaged and documents were reported to have been taken away. What secrets they may contain is a matter of speculation. They are likely to fuel the Iranians' anger and may cause embarrassment to the British government if revealed. Aware of the 1961 Vienna Convention on Diplomatic Relations, the Iranian foreign ministry expressed regret and promised to protect the British diplomatic staff. But Ali Larijani, speaker of Iran's parliament, said that the student protesters' action reflected the anti-British sentiment in Iran. Other Iranian MPs expressed similar views. The British government had little choice but to withdraw its staff, and it ordered the closure of the Iranian embassy in London within 48 hours.

Britain's announcement falls short of a complete break, but relations between the two countries have sunk perhaps to the lowest point in more than three decades. The British Foreign Secretary William Hague says that he wants to remain engaged with Tehran on the nuclear issue and on human rights, an astonishing statement to make.

Iran is no longer the same country as it was just after the overthrow of Shah Reza Pahlavi, America's close ally and widely detested by his own countrymen. There is not the same religious fervor in Iranian society. The structure that now rules Iran has evolved over three decades. No doubt there are factions and power struggles, but the hierarchy of clerics led by Ayatollah Khamenei and an elected president, parliament and the judiciary, brings some stability in the country.

Violence during and after Iran's disputed presidential election in 2009 showed that the regime can use considerable force when faced with a serious challenge. Accusations of Western powers backing opposition forces appear to unite the country's structure. At the same time, Iran has emerged as a major Shi'a power in a predominantly Sunni region which is led by Saudi Arabia. Pressures over centuries have made the Iranians rather like the Chinese. They can wait for a long time before giving a typically Persian response. Last month's IAEA report accusing Tehran of operating a nuclear weapons program began the latest escalation. The timing of the report looked expedient, coming immediately after the overthrow of Libya's Muammar Gaddafi and at a time when the conflict in Syria was intensifying.

As the Middle East threatens to explode and the crisis between Iran and the West escalates, one question which policymakers in London and Washington do not seem to ask themselves is: What lies behind Iran's deep suspicion of the West? Writing in the Independent, Robert Fisk reminded us of the essential answer. A country humiliated and pushed again and again is a country radicalized and distrustful. Iranians have been humiliated repeatedly, their resources stolen and they blame the West. In 1941, the British and Soviet armies invaded the country for oil and a supply line to the Allied forces in the Second World War. Then a plot by the British intelligence agency MI6 and the American CIA overthrew Iran's democratically elected government in 1953.

For more than a quarter century thereafter, the West enabled Shah Reza Pahlavi to rule the country with an iron fist. He was finally deposed in the 1979 Revolution. The West then helped Iraq's Saddam Hussein, who invaded Iran, in a war in which as many as a million Iranians died or were wounded and chemical weapons were used by the Iraqi army on Iranian troops. More than two decades on, we know where the recent sanctions are coming from. Killings of scientists and academics and mysterious explosions in different parts of Iran are much more difficult to explain. In Britain, the regulators have threatened Iran's Press TV broadcasts with closure. Iran's national character has been shaped by many traumatic experiences for which the country holds the West responsible.

Explosive drivers in international relations such as these have a high price tag. Many diplomats seem to know it, politicians not quite. The world after the Cold War is driven by crises largely because rough politics has sidelined skilled diplomacy. We live in a world where leaders are many, leadership is scarce. Having spent their moral and material capital, war is an increasingly preferred option for declining powers. History of savage conflicts follows an all too familiar pattern.

CHAPTER FOUR:

GLOBALIZATION AND THE FALLOUT

LIVING WITH THE HEGEMON

July 17, 2012

Recent wars from Libya to Afghanistan and Pakistan in a region of vast natural wealth and strategic importance highlight a phenomenon as old as humanity. Iraq and Libya had oil, but their leaders were longtime foes of the United States, now the world's lone hegemon. Saddam Hussein allied with the Soviet Union before its demise, so did Muammar Gaddafi. They both displayed stubbornness and were ready to drop the American dollar as the oil currency before bigger players like China and India dared. Saddam and Gaddafi ruled with an iron hand their state systems that were brittle. They were too independent for their own good.

Saudi Arabia and tiny Arab emirates such as Bahrain and Qatar, on the other hand, are punching above their weights. Wealthy and dictatorial, their rulers accommodate the hegemon's interests. These rulers sell their oil and amass petrodollars which they spend in vast quantities on weapons and consumer goods from the industrialized world led by the hegemon. It is a far more agreeable relationship.

The hegemon is thus left with states of two more categories of significant kind. In one category is Iran since the 1979 Revolution, Syria since the 1963 Ba'athist coup, and Sudan. The hegemon intervenes seeking to overthrow uncooperative regimes by diplomatic, economic and military means. In the second category are China, Russia and, to a lesser degree, India, where even the world's lone hegemon has limits. Beyond these categories are the discarded—completely failed entities like Somalia, Ethiopia, Mali, where utterly poor and miserable people live. The hegemon and satellites have not a care in the world for the welfare of such people, except sending drones or troops from neighboring client states to kill those described as "terrorists." What desperate poverty and misery lead to has no space within the realm of this thinking.

Plato's Republic, written around 380 BC, has a dialogue between Socrates and Glaucon about civilized society. They discuss how a society develops from primitive to higher levels of civilization. Trades and occupations multiply and population grows. The next stage of development, according to Socrates, is an increase in wealth that results in war, because an enlarged society wants even more for consumption. Plato's explanation is fundamental to understanding the causes of war. This is how empires rise, military and economic power being essential to further their aims. A relevant section in the Republic reads:

We shall have to enlarge our state again. Our healthy state is no longer big enough; its size must be enlarged to make room for a multitude of occupations none of which is concerned with necessaries. There will be hunters and fishermen, and there will be artists, sculptors, painters and musicians. There will be poets with their following of reciters, actors, chorus-trainers, and producers; there will be manufacturers of domestic equipment of all sorts, especially those concerned with women's dress and make-up.

Nearly two and a half millennia after Plato, Antonio Negri and Michael Hardt offered a Marxist vision of the twenty-first century in their book, Empire. Their core argument in the book published in 2000 was that globalization did not mean erosion of sovereignty, but a set of new power relationships in the form of national and supranational institutions like the United Nations, the European Union and the World Trade Organization. According to Negri and Hardt, unlike European imperialism based on the notions of national sovereignty and territorial cohesion, empire now is a concept in the garb of globalization of production, trade and communication. It has no definitive political center and no territorial limits. The concept is all pervading, so the "enemy" must now be someone who poses a threat to the entire system—a "terrorist" entity to be dealt with by force. Written in the mid-1990s, Empire got it right, as subsequent events testify.

The United States occupied "a privileged position in Empire" depicted by Negri and Hardt. Its privileges did not necessarily arise from its "similarities to the old European imperialist powers." They derived from the assertion of "American exceptionalism." From the early days of its formal constitution, the founders of the United States had believed that they were creating "a new Empire with open, expanding frontiers," where power would be distributed in networks. More than two centuries later, the idea had become global. The presidency of George W. Bush was a powerful militaristic expression of America's will.

Like terrorism, the term "empire" is often used disparagingly by those on the left and the right. The emergence of the United States and the Soviet Union as the two greatest powers after the Second World War offered contrasting models. Advocates of each accused the other of being an empire, meaning a large population comprising many nationalities in distant territories living under subjugation or exploitation.

Different concepts of empire have existed through history. For centuries, the term referred to states that considered themselves successors to the Roman Empire, but later it came to be applied to non-European monarchies such as the Empire of China or the Mughal Empire. Most empires in history came into being as a result of a militarily strong state taking control of weaker ones. The result in each case was an enlarged, more powerful political union, before its eventual decline.

The dissolution of the Soviet bloc in the late 1980s and early 1990s was a blow against the idea of ruling an empire by brute force. Suddenly, the floodgates opened for rapid globalization and expansion of the markets to places that had previously been in the Soviet domain. Capitalism could reach where it had not been before, from newly independent countries in eastern Europe to Soviet-style economies in Asia and Africa. Two decades later, the West was to hit the most serious crisis since the Great Depression. It was brought about by a combination of impudence after the West's Cold War triumph, false sense of moral superiority and belief in its power to destroy and recreate nations at will.

Norwegian scholar Johan Galtung, regarded as the father of conflict and peace studies, said in 2004 something that is a fitting definition of the term "empire." He described it as "a system of unequal exchanges between the center and the periphery." An empire "legitimizes relationships between exploiters and exploited economically, killers and victims militarily, dominators and dominated politically and alienators and alienated culturally." Galtung observed that the U.S. empire "provides a complete configuration, articulated in a statement by a Pentagon planner." The Pentagon planner in question was Lt. Col. Ralph Peters:

The de facto role of the United States Armed Forces will be to keep the world safe for our economy and open to our cultural assault. To those ends, we will do a fair amount of killing. (Fighting for the Future: Will America Triumph? 1999, 141)

The American defense planner's confession was as revealing as it was terrifying. Economic interest and cultural domination are interwoven in imperial thinking, driven by its simplistic logic. Imperial powers are expansionist by nature, always inclined to enlarge territories they control. What lies behind their ambition is access to more and more resources—energy, minerals, raw materials and markets to trade. Imperial behavior drives a great power to expand its domain of direct control or influence by military and other means to territories that have resources and a certain cultural symmetry with the center. The greater the cultural symmetry, the better for the hegemon.

How Capitalism Flopped

November 7, 2011

In the struggle against global laissez faire capitalism that has brought the current economic collapse, protesters won an important victory last week in Britain, while stalemate continued in Greece. The alliance between the church, the main financial district called the City of London and Mayor Boris Johnson against the Occupy London protest crumbled. They had threatened legal action to remove peaceful demonstrators occupying an area near the London Stock Exchange for several weeks. Legal moves against the protesters might have led to police action and violence. In particular, the readiness of St Paul's Cathedral, the seat of the Bishop of London, to go to High Court split the church. Senior priests began to resign, signaling a crisis for the British establishment. Facing a growing sense of disquiet over possible use of force to remove peaceful demonstrators, the Corporation of London and St Paul's Cathedral dropped the threat of immediate legal action.

In Greece, Prime Minister George Papandreou threw down the gauntlet to the two most powerful member-states of the European Union—Germany and France. To salvage the Greek economy and the European currency, they had agreed to finance a huge rescue plan, involving the International Monetary Fund and other sources, only days before. In the face of widespread demonstrations against draconian cuts in wages and public services and rumors of a possible military coup, the Greek prime minister announced a referendum on the European Union rescue package.

Initially, the Greek cabinet gave its backing to the referendum plan, but the leaders of other EU member-states were furious. Deep political splits began to appear in Greece's body politic. Germany and France have a lot to lose if Greece should default on its massive debt. Any government in Athens must have the people's mandate to implement draconian austerity measures. Already, Greek people have started to take matters in their own hands. Timing was of essence for Prime Minister Papandreou. First he agreed on a mega rescue deal with other European partners. When such a deal looked certain, he returned home and announced his referendum plan. European leaders, opposition politicians in Greece, even in his own Socialist Party, were surprised and angry. What might have been a straightforward move to secure a people's mandate, provided the timing was right, seemed to be an opportunistic attempt to save his government.

Chancellor Angela Merkel of Germany, leading paymaster of the euro bailout package, bluntly told Papandreou to accept the rescue deal with all conditions attached—or get out. Such warnings were bound to cause widespread offense in Greece, not least because the country had been under German occupation during the Second War. At the G20 summit in the French Mediterranean city of Cannes, European leaders waited to welcome the Chinese leader, Hu Jintao, hoping that China would contribute to the euro bailout. Hu's response: "To resolve the eurozone's debt crisis, Europe still needs to rely on itself." The Chinese are shrewd investors. How did we get to this point? The question is posed frequently, though rarely answered truthfully.

The current globalization phase, beginning at the end of the Cold War around 1990, extended the markets across state boundaries. The movement of money, goods and services on a massive scale across national boundaries required regulations, but they also had to be relaxed in ways not seen before to facilitate the ease of transfer. The Nobel Prize winning Columbia University economist Joseph Stiglitz points out that the "driver" behind this phase of globalization is corporate interests.

Many transnational corporations are bigger than most national economies. Powerful corporations export not only goods and services, but also a certain culture of borrowing, cheap labor and money. Corporate interests are fundamentally linked to consumption, for profits are driven by consumption. Corporate investments have flown to destinations of cheap labor and weak unions—China and Southeast Asia, India, Turkey, Southern European countries and South America. Factories in the United States and Western Europe have closed, new plants have spread in Asia and South America. Acceleration in this phenomenon in the last two decades has resulted in massive job losses in the industrialized world. Most products bought by Western consumers now come from the emerging economies.

Corporate profits have steadily grown, but the overall purchasing power of Western consumers has declined to alarming levels, caused by rising unemployment and shrinking incomes of those still in work. Government revenues, too, have been declining in the West, which has demonstrated a propensity to spend enormous sums of money on wars abroad and to cut public services at home. For too long, consumers and governments tried to maintain the status quo by borrowing money at artificially low interest rates and cheap goods manufactured abroad. Loans secured on the real state to finance the lifestyle in the West sent property prices sky high. The crash was inevitable.

The case of the Greek tragedy is stark, but Greece is not alone. For a long time, its people have not been paying taxes they should have been paying. The country has been borrowing to maintain living standards, pay wages of government employees, to hold events like the Athens Olympics in 2004. The party had to be over one day–and that day has arrived. Less than a quarter century after long celebrations of victory over communism began in the West, capitalism has flopped.

INDIA'S NEOLIBERAL ELITE

December 19, 2008

Tragedy and trauma magnify a nation's awareness or lack thereof. The events surrounding the Mumbai carnage have revealed certain aspects of India's collective psyche that provide food for thought and perhaps a lesson to learn. The country had already suffered a wave of mindless bombings and targeted attacks on Muslim and Christian minorities recently. That the killings in Mumbai by Muslim gunmen, whose victims included dozens of fellow Muslims, did not lead to further retribution was an achievement. So weary was the country of the possibility of another disastrous turn of events.

On Indian television channels, though, there was plenty of heat and theater in debates. Voices of reason appeared to drown in high-pitched rhetoric from a handful of guests—socialites and self-styled commentators. They were in competition for space with politicians, academics and journalists of the more established ranks. Ex-model, now socialite and author, Shobha De, described as India's answer to Jackie Collins, known for her erotic novels, lambasted politicians for "failures" that led to the bloodbath. "Enough is enough," she screamed. India's leading English news channel, NDTV, responded by naming an entire episode "Enough is Enough." Participants had a field day attacking the government and politicians. Those who begged that the fiery rhetoric be toned down had little chance of succeeding until the heat was exhausted.

There were loud calls to teach Pakistan a lesson. The Mumbai attack was described as "India's 9/11." Participants demanded that India launch military raids inside Pakistan to destroy militant bases—rather like America using pilotless aircraft that regularly kill many more innocent civilians than militants. Simi Garewal, a movie actress of the 1960s and 1970s, later to host her own talk show, was not going to be left behind. Look at how America retaliated after September 11, 2001, she argued, and no one has dared to harm it since. Even more grotesque was praise for Israel's behavior from a guest.

A recent discussion program on "Hindu terror" turned to the possibility of Hindu fundamentalism affecting some in the Indian armed forces. The issue was how the military can remain unaffected by a phenomenon that exists in the wider society. When a U.S.-educated academic of Indian descent tried to speak, he was abruptly told by a participant that there would not be a word said against the army. I have said before that these comments came from a small group of India's neoliberal elite—smart, well-spoken and aggressive. These neoliberals undoubtedly love their country, but their worldview is as misinformed as their remedies are perilous. They boast of India's military might, but fail to understand that Pakistan, like India, also has nuclear weapons. Before both countries became nuclear powers, India's bigger armed forces meant the balance of power was in its favor. With nuclear deterrence, Pakistan is now equal to India. A basic knowledge of the doctrine of "Mutually Assured Destruction" would be enough to counter the foolish proposition of war on Pakistan.

Equally careless and dangerous were claims about the American retaliation against Afghanistan and the illegal invasion of Iraq, which, it was said, had prevented further attacks on the United States. Such claims are little more than regurgitated rhetoric of George W. Bush to begin with. The facts tell a very different story. Terrorist attacks on U.S. mainland are neither frequent, nor have they always originated from outside. Before September 11, 2001, the previous attack by external forces on American mainland was the car bombing of the World Trade Center in 1993. Two years later, a homegrown American bomber, Timothy McVeigh, devastated a large government building in Oklahoma City, killing about 170 people and wounding more than 850 others.

The 9/11 attacks came six years after the Oklahoma City bombing by McVeigh and one hopes nothing like that happens again. Meanwhile, 5,000 American soldiers have died and tens of thousands have been injured and traumatized in Afghanistan and Iraq. Hundreds of thousands of Afghans and Iraqis have perished. Millions have been made homeless and displaced. Many have been abducted, tortured and thrown into notorious prisons like Guantanamo. The hatred for the Bush administration is widespread. From the Palestinian Territories through Saudi Arabia, Iraq and Afghanistan to Pakistan, India and elsewhere— the overall balance sheet of George W. Bush is deeply in the red, even without considering the world economic slump.

Heaping praise on Israel's conduct from the television studios of Bombay and Delhi has no relation with realities in the Middle East. Despite its huge military superiority and brutal tactics, Israel has failed to tame the Palestinian rebellion. One-and-a-half million Palestinians in Gaza, two-thirds of them registered with the United Nations as refugees, live in desperate conditions, under an Israeli blockade. Even Israelis are alarmed at their government's tactics and the deteriorating situation all around their country.

Israel's military superiority is maintained by more than three billion dollars of American money every year. The nuclear weapons which Israel first developed in the late 1960s may have deterred its Arab enemies in the 1973 war and afterwards. Today, Israel faces a different threat. It comes from the mass of alienated humanity encircling Israel that nuclear weapons cannot counter. A country of Israel's size in the midst of Arab neighbors cannot use weapons of mass destruction without consequences for itself. All of which tells us that members of the relatively small westernized, but ill-informed, neoliberal elite of India would benefit from the reserve of morality and wisdom the country has accumulated over its long history. The lesson to learn is that thoughtless talk without considering the consequences is dangerous.

INDIAN ELECTIONS

May 23, 2009

The results of India's month-long general election will be analyzed in the coming days and months for their political shift and possible effects on the country's domestic and foreign policies. It is worth looking at some notable aspects to emerge and what they mean, for they will be indicators of the likely conduct of India and what to expect in the next few years.

The United Progressive Alliance led by the Congress Party has retained power. Its performance has defied many predictions. With over 200 seats won by Congress alone, the alliance finished up just short of an absolute majority in the 543 contested seats for the lower house of parliament. Such a performance is enough to attract support from smaller parties. The governing alliance should have a safe passage through the next five years. The Congress leadership will be relieved for two other reasons. First, the governing coalition will not have to depend on the Marxists as had been the case in the last parliament. Second, the Marxists themselves have suffered heavy reverses, and their strength is much diminished. To a considerable degree, this outcome is of their own making. They turned on themselves as the 2009 election approached. Their gamble to confront the governing alliance over India's relations with the West and over economic policy failed.

The revival of Congress in northern India, once the citadel which gave it control over power, after years of decay is another remarkable feature of this election. Muslims and groups at the bottom rung of India's Hindu caste system that once formed its core support have returned to Congress in significant numbers. In state after state, including Uttar Pradesh, Rajasthan, Madhya Pradesh, Punjab, Haryana and Delhi, Congress won more seats than the most optimistic forecasts before the vote. Even in Gujarat and Madhya Pradesh, strongholds of the Hindu nationalist BJP, the Congress-led alliance did better than had been expected. Only

Bihar and Orissa, where regional leaders were in power, bucked the trend, depriving Congress of any chance of making significant inroads. The victory of the United Progressive Alliance led by Sonia Gandhi and Prime Minister Man Mohan Singh has come despite widespread anger and criticism of the government following the Mumbai massacre in November 2008. As evidence mounted that a Pakistan-based group was behind the attack, there were calls for military reprisal by India, similar to the American response after 9/11. The BJP accused the government and the prime minister in particular of weakness. Despite the rhetoric that mirrored the nation's anger, the decision to refrain from acting impulsively against a nuclear-armed rival was judicious, and a war with Pakistan was avoided. Polling went off peacefully throughout India over an extended period. The governing alliance benefited as Muslims and other minorities drew toward Congress. Those leaning toward extreme and caste-based politics paid the price.

These are comforting developments for much of the international community, especially the United States and Europe. They know who they will be dealing with over the next five years. Man Mohan Singh remains India's prime minister, with Sonia Gandhi the power holding it all together. The emergence of a new tier of young, educated leaders, including Rahul Gandhi, a political novice, will be viewed in western capitals with satisfaction. They will see the development as a sign of an emerging new generation which is pro-West.

Such a young generation of leaders is necessary as India takes on an increasingly higher profile globally. There is a new administration in the United States and a different government is likely in Britain after polls due within a year. In the present global economic meltdown, emerging powers like India and China must readjust with new realities. The challenges require continuity, as well as correction. People like the former Under-Secretary general of the United Nations, Shashi Tharoor, just elected to parliament, and Rahul Gandhi are the new faces of India on the international stage. In a turbulent region at a time of multiple crises, India has emerged after the 2009 election prepared to face both challenges and opportunities awaiting the country.

ON CAPITALISM AND RESPONSIBILITY

January 29, 2012

A few days before the annual gathering of business and political elites at the World Economic Forum at Davos, the British Prime Minister David Cameron set out his vision of capitalism that is popular and responsible. At a time of acute crisis, Cameron put up a staunch defense of capitalism. He asserted his belief that open markets and free enterprise were the best imaginable force for improving human wealth and happiness. He described them as the engine of progress to lift people out of poverty and give them opportunity. "When open markets work properly," he said, "they create morality, because there is something for something."

Can today's capitalism be responsible? Can it be popular in the sense that people in great numbers embrace it and benefit in a fair way? Distinguished British Marxist historian Eric Hobsbawm does not think so. In a sharp critique, Hobsbawm made the point that capitalism as practiced in the last 40 years was all about growth and profit and not much else. The "trickle-down theory" associated with free enterprise and open markets has failed. We have again entered an era of mass unemployment, poverty, malnutrition, disease and wars. The root cause of inequalities lies in the fact that the powerful in society have engineered systems that suck most of the wealth up rather than allow it to trickle down. Capitalism has become a distorted and twisted version of Adam Smith's original idea.

Technological advances, particularly since the 1970s, have massively and rapidly altered the capitalist system in one crucial respect. As Hobsbawm suggested, computers and robots have created a large surplus of people around the globe. And capitalism, which is about growth, profit and speed of production, is unable and unwilling to deal with the surplus of humans. Agriculture, automobile and shipbuilding industries once employed workers in their millions. Today, they employ a tiny proportion of the population. Feudalism, which preceded modern capitalism, and communism, which competed with it, engaged many more people. Communism failed because, despite all its idealism, it was conservative, nationalistic and coercive. The capitalist system suffers from the same type of orthodoxy today. It is polluted by narrow individualism and nationalism.

In Britain, with business closures and job cuts in the private and public sectors, three million unemployed and many more underemployed or simply staying home, Prime Minister David Cameron's message to people is, "Don't complain about welfare cuts, go and find work." Profit-driven manufacturing practices and outsourcing have brought about a collapse on the job market. To tell vulnerable people to "go and find work" is a contradiction in itself. It is a serious dereliction of responsibility by politicians who are viewed by many to have contributed to the present crisis.

Once fertile landscape of capitalism, the United States and Europe, is barren. The race for control of energy resources is increasingly desperate, affecting foes and friends alike. The new cold war around Iran and the Persian Gulf has escalated to a point where China, India and Russia, three main Eastern powers, are drawn into open confrontation with America and the European Union. The Eastern powers are refusing to obey the Western sanctions regime against Iran, driven by U.S. law and outside the United Nations. Washington's offer to compensate the Iranian supplies lost with extra crude from Saudi Arabia and other U.S. allies will inevitably give the United States more leverage on energy supplies to China and India. These countries find the offer unacceptable, for it could be a trap.

The world's only superpower is no longer credible if it cannot force others to follow it. However, the scenario is before us, because capitalism has become irrational and sick. It is looking to transfer the cost of securing its own interests to others who are not prepared to accept that cost. In a candid admission, the Chinese ambassador in Britain, Liu Xiaoming, said that his government had to think of nearly half of China's 1.3 billion population living in the countryside, and more than 150 million people earning as little as a dollar a day.

Like China's overall growth in percentage terms, India's growth is also impressive. The proportion of Indians living below the poverty line has dropped from about 60 to 40 percent in two decades, but the story it tells is partial. The latest available World Bank data shows nearly half a billion Indians living below the international poverty line of 1.25 dollars per day, and their number is not falling. Half of the children are underweight and 45 percent under the age of three suffer from malnutrition.

Inequalities have worsened alarmingly while corporate predators like Wal-Mart make an aggressive push into China and India. The gap between India's richest and poorest states is nearly three-and-a-half times. As a result of government policies, there have been dramatic rises in the prices of hybrid seeds and fertilizers. In a country where 60 percent of the population is directly or indirectly dependent on agriculture, more than 200,000 farmers in debt have committed suicide in the last 15 years. And the number continues to rise. The Indian government's recent move that would have given unprecedented access to mega retail houses like Wal-Mart to the middle-class market, amid widely feared consequences for small farmers and merchants, had to be put off, at least temporarily, following a huge national outcry.

In their anxiety to move India from the Soviet-style economic model to the U.S. model, and haste to transform the country into a superpower, successive governments in Delhi have been tempted to go to very significant lengths. But the capitalist model has become distorted and twisted. Having wreaked havoc at home, free-market capitalism seeks to penetrate societies where many more vulnerable people need greater protection. Only governments acting responsibly can provide that safeguard.

BATTLE FOR WORLD ENERGY RESOURCES

January 30, 2012

The brinkmanship between the West and Iran over Tehran's nuclear program has further escalated in the last week. First came the European Union's announcement of a ban on the import of Iranian oil from July 2012. It was the last straw, and prompted the Iranian authorities to announce via Press TV that Parliament was about to pass a law banning oil exports to the EU immediately. "Less than 20 percent of Iran's crude oil is currently being exported to Europe and Iran has no problem in selling its oil to a market other than the EU." According to Press TV, Managing Director of the National Iranian Oil Company (NIOC) Ahmad Qalebani said that crude oil prices could reach $150 a barrel in the aftermath of the EU sanctions on Iran's oil exports. He further warned that "global economic and business blocs will experience tremendous shocks because of the embargo on Tehran, and the West will suffer the most from the measure." Meanwhile, Majlis is due to "debate a bill this week that would cut off oil supplies to the EU in a matter of days, in response to the 27-member bloc's decision to stop importing crude oil from Iran as of July."

The EU embargo was in line with a law which President Obama signed last month. The fact that, using U.S. domestic law, the measure threatens punitive sanctions against any country doing business with Iran was too much for China and India, a long-time ally of Washington. Iranian oil is crucial for the Indian economy. India's frustration at the Western moves to control its foreign and domestic economic policy exploded into the open. Indian officials pointedly refused to deny a report by DEBKAfile, Israel's intelligence news service, that India would pay for Iranian oil in gold. And India's Finance Minister Pranab Mukherjee said bluntly: "We import 110 million tonnes of crude per year. We will not decrease imports from Iran. Iran is an important country for India despite U.S. and European sanctions on Iran."

Earlier, the U.S. Treasury Secretary Timothy Geithner had failed in his mission to persuade Beijing to cut oil supplies from Iran. Geithner was told in Beijing that China was opposed to sanctions beyond those imposed by the United Nations. "Iran is an extremely big oil supplier to China, and we hope that China's oil imports won't be affected, because this is needed for our development," Zhai Jun, China's vice foreign minister, told a news conference. And he continued that "we oppose applying pressure and sanctions, because these approaches won't solve the problems. They never have. We hope that these unilateral sanctions will not affect China's interests." These reactions from China and India have had a sobering effect on Europe. As the Iranian parliament debates the bill on banning oil exports to the European Union, Germany has now urged Tehran to "exercise restraint."

The escalation of sanctions by the United States and the European Union outside the United Nations system, and attempts to force others to toe the line, amount to an open act of war. China, India and others will see them as illegal and a clear violation of their sovereign right to formulate their own policies.

Once fertile landscape of capitalism, the United States and Europe, lies barren. The race for control of energy resources has become increasingly desperate, affecting foes and friends alike. And the new cold war, involving military buildup, around Iran and the Gulf has escalated to a point where China, India and Russia, three main Eastern powers, are drawn into open confrontation with America and the European Union.

Sarkozy's France

April 1, 2012

Toulouse, Europe's aerospace hub in the southwest of France, has hit the headlines for the wrong reasons. A 23-year-old French citizen of Algerian origin, Mohammed Merah, went on a shooting spree last month, killing seven people and terrorizing a million residents for 10 days before a police sniper's bullet ended his life. Among his victims were three unarmed soldiers, a rabbi and three children at a Jewish school. According to prosecutors privy to negotiations with Merah during the 30-hour siege where he met his end, his only regret was "not having claimed more victims." He reportedly said that he was proud of having "brought France to its knees."

Mohammed Merah had many more years to live had it not been for his final act. Life was, however, not important to him. He claimed to have been motivated by the Palestinians' plight, the presence of French troops in Afghanistan and the law banning the full veil in France. These issues challenge the conscience of many people, but a young man depriving fellow citizens of life, and throwing away his own, cannot constitute a solution.

What is known about Merah's short life does not suggest that he was particularly religious. He frequented bars and nightclubs in his home town. He had displayed other imperfections of a disturbed youth—petty crime, driving without license and fistfights. In this light, Merah's assertion of belonging to al Qaeda is more likely to have been an exaggeration or empty boast than a serious claim to infamy. It has prompted some sections of the media to run with speculation, without much evidence, that Merah was affiliated to al Qaeda and the Taliban. French police are investigating whether he visited Afghanistan, but indications of any ideological twist are thin, for Mohamed Merah was not a devout Muslim.

We should mourn Merah's victims and express sympathy for their relatives and friends whose lives have been shattered. It was a needless act of revenge on people whose only fault was to belong to the French armed forces, or to the Jewish community. Worse, his victims included children. Thus if it is right to condemn the recent massacre of innocent Afghans by an American soldier in Kandahar, then it is also right to condemn the killings in Toulouse. That children were among the victims in both places is particularly distressing and requires reflection on our part.

Like the context of Kandahar, there is a context of Toulouse. Kandahar is one of Afghanistan's Pashtun-dominated provinces, the stronghold of Taliban-led resistance to foreign military forces, who regularly launch night raids in local residents' homes to hunt for men described as Taliban, their militant supporters and sympathizers. The American soldier, St. Sgt. Robert Bales, charged with 17 murders after the Kandahar massacre, was flown out to the United States for possible military trial that could take years. Mohamed Merah, born and raised in deprived immigrant neighborhoods in France, was condemned as the guilty killer, his life ended by a sniper's bullet.

A country of just under 65 million people, France has a 20 percent immigrant population. Many came from French-speaking Africa, or were born and raised in France. Unemployment among them is high. Living conditions in immigrant neighborhoods are harsh. There are areas where petty crime is rampant, reinforced by economic failure. Merah's crime cannot be condoned by these factors. But he was one of the many to have become disconnected from French society, where the anti-immigrant and anti-Muslim sentiments are virulent. With one in seven French voters projected to support the far-right Front National in the first round of the coming presidential election, politicians have not hesitated to make an issue of the race.

Even President Nicolas Sarkozy, son of a Hungarian immigrant family, says there are too many foreigners in the country, and that he would reduce their numbers if he wins a second term. The September 11, 2001 attacks were compared to the Japanese air assault on Pearl Harbor during the Second World War. For Western politicians dressed up with ambition and agenda, 9/11 has become the benchmark for discussion on any militant act by a non-state group or individual. Sarkozy is the latest to jump on the 9/11 bandwagon.

In the midst of deep economic and social problems, Sarkozy faces an uphill election battle against the Socialist candidate Francois Hollande. With support for the far-right running around 15 percent, the real battle is for that vote in the second round after the Front National candidate, Marine Le Pen, has been eliminated in the first. In a frantic bid for that vote, Sarkozy's campaign has been moving to the right, steadily and dangerously.

The immigrant population of France feels targeted by a series of new laws. A combination of coercive measures to force people of non-European origins to conform to the "French way of life," socioeconomic problems, lack of opportunities and perceived loss of identity is causing a boomerang effect in French society. It is forcing young individuals from vulnerable communities to go on a luckless search for identity and causes which they do not fully comprehend. Mohamed Merah, too, was a victim of this phenomenon.

What's Left?

April 15, 2012

The public suicide of 77-year-old pharmacist Demitris Christoulas a short distance from the parliament building in Athens and the outpouring of grief and anger reveal the trauma and desperation in Greek society in the midst of an economic crisis. In a handwritten note before he shot himself in the head, Christoulas complained that the government had made it impossible for him to survive on the pension he had paid into for 35 years. The note on his body said, "I find no other solution than a dignified end before I start searching through the trash for food."

To get a rescue package for its economy and to keep its place in the euro zone, the Greek government has slashed wages and retirement pensions by as much as 25 percent. With the unemployment rate exceeding 20 percent, Greece faces a national ordeal. Last year, the government admitted that suicides had risen by 40 percent over the previous two years. A day before Christoulas ended his life, an Italian woman of 78 in Sicily had jumped from the balcony of her third-floor apartment. Her monthly pension had been cut from 800 to 600 euros and she could take no more. Her son said, "The government is making us all poor, apart from the wealthy, who they don't touch, in contrast with us workers and small businessmen who are struggling with heavy debts." A week before, a businessman tried to commit suicide by setting himself alight outside a tax office. He had lost his appeal against a claim of unpaid tax. And a 27-year-old construction worker of Moroccan descent set himself alight, because he had not been paid wages for four months.

Thus an alarming trend, first seen among India's debt-ridden farmers in the 1990s, has spread to the European Union, where citizens have begun to end their lives because of crushing poverty and utter hopelessness. There is a feeling that rich will become richer at the expense of poor, that governments will either side with the wealthy, or be impotent in the face of powerful institutions determined to force economic reengineering on nations that will bring the greatest pain to the greatest number of people.

The age-old social contract between the state and its citizens is in an unprecedented crisis. Philosopher Jean Jacques Rousseau implied in his eighteenth-century work, A Discourse On Inequality, that natural inequality, meaning disparity between human strength and weakness, is established by nature. But moral inequality is based on a kind of convention that is established, or at least authorized, by the consent of citizens. Today, the system of privileges, which some enjoy to the prejudice of others, is fighting for legitimacy. Those who are privileged are "more rich, more honored, more powerful and in a position to extract obedience."

Human evolution has been an epic struggle against moral inequality, which inevitably leads to accumulation of wealth and power and abuse of both. That monumental struggle is at a crucial juncture. On one end are forces of unrestrained capitalism that have been in the ascendancy since the collapse of communism. On the other, expressions of mass opposition in the form of Arab awakening and occupy movements in the American and European continents.

People's movements are usurped by the very forces they were supposed to fight. The prospect looks more bleak and bloody. To pessimists, the contest between the corporate interests, international institutions and ruling elites on one hand and the citizens on the other is increasingly one-sided. The feeling of disenfranchisement has spread to the north. Modern capitalism has created conditions not unlike those found under communism, which allowed party bosses and bureaucrats to control the population. Democratic centralism, sanctified by Lenin as "freedom for discussion, unity of action" at the Tenth Party Congress in 1933 may look obsolete a quarter century after Soviet communism collapsed. But corporate businesses and international financial institutions, working in harmony with politicians and other members of the ruling elites using state instruments, have gained unprecedented control over vast numbers of citizens today.

The pyramid of power is intact. Social democrats once provided an alternative with a conscience to extreme rightwing monetarism. But they have all but surrendered to the neo-capitalist theory based only on growth and the idea that the one and only social responsibility of business is to make profit. Political labels of Left and Right have become meaningless, and autocratic instincts of capitalism of today mirror those of communism of the days gone by.

THE TIDE IS TURNING IN EUROPE

May 21, 2012

Recent elections in France and Greece have generated a good deal of comment, suggesting that the years of center-right governance in Europe may be coming to an end. The defeat of President Nicolas Sarkozy of France by the Socialist candidate Francois Hollande, and the collapse in Greece of political parties that allowed unrestrained capitalism and chaos to take hold, are major developments. Whether they represent a turning-point likely to return Western Europe to social democracy cannot be taken for granted yet.

Public opinion has become radicalized to an alarming degree. European societies are undergoing a process of atomization as confidence in mainstream political parties and their leaders collapses. In the midst of a severe continental crisis, millions upon millions of people feel that their leaders are both unwilling and unable to look for solutions to help the most vulnerable. The masses have become disgusted with professional politicians after giving them many opportunities. Recent national and regional elections in Greece, France and Germany are proof of voters walking away from mainstream parties whose political labels and programs are deceptive.

The same trend has been repeated in the recent local elections in Britain. Unfortunately, when a government loses, the victor picks up where the defeated left. Callous disregard of the masses, and obsession with the accountants' jargon of "balancing the books," are behind the austerity imposed on ordinary citizens throughout the European continent. The result is the collapse of traditional politics and the rise of groups on the extremes.

This phenomenon across Europe mirrors what has long been happening in the United States. The difference is that in Europe the coercive power of supranational financial institutions, supported by the United States, is being applied with extraordinary ferocity and haste. It goes against the postwar liberal consensus developed following the devastation of the two world wars in the last century.

The most traumatic events are taking place in Greece. The fall of the Panhellenic Socialist Movement (PASOK) from governance to near insignificance, and the collapse of the New Democracy Party vote by a third, in the recent general election are dramatic. One of the consequences is the rise of new political groups, most notably Syriza, vehemently opposed to the austerity package which Germany, the wealthiest European country, insists upon.

The German chancellor, Angela Merkel, has her own domestic compulsions. Germany's public opinion is strongly against bailing other countries out of the crisis. But in refusing to yield on harsh cuts, and work for economic growth instead, the German chancellor has created the impression that she does not recognize the Greek people's democratic choice. The appearance of diktats from Bonn is a highly sensitive issue, for memories of Nazi occupation of Greece during the Second World War are still alive among many Greeks. They may be one of the poorest member-states in the European Union, but are proud of their history and civilization.

The Greek electorate's refusal to accept harsh cuts any more, reflected in the country's extraordinarily polarization, made the formation of a coalition government impossible. Reports of the German chancellor telling Greece to hold a referendum on whether Athens wanted to retain the euro currency added fuel to the fire and those reports had to be denied. The coming election in June will in effect be a referendum on Greece's continuing presence in the euro area. Otherwise, the country will walk away from the straightjacket which eurozone has become, prompting a default on its debt payments and causing a financial "calamity," as many free marketeers have been predicting with passion.

The past decade has been one of retreat for social democratic politics in Europe. From Scandinavian countries in the north to Italy and Greece in the south, the political right has been dominant across the continent. However, just when old social democrats looked utterly defeated, new forces of the left are beginning to come forward. They have begun to fight back and the tide has started to turn.

As long as Chancellor Merkel of Germany had an ally in Nicolas Sarkozy as the president of France, the duo dominated. Now, however, Greece is not the only European Union member in crisis and Merkel stands severely weakened by at least two factors. One is the defiance of the Greek people. The other, even more decisive, is the defeat of Sarkozy in the French presidential election. Along with Greece, France too goes to the polls for the National Assembly in June, when the domination of the French right is almost certain to end. At home, the defeat of Merkel's party in Germany's most populous region, North Rhine Westphalia, by the Social Democrats is a major jolt against her center-right coalition.

So the tide is turning in Europe and the left is emerging from the wilderness years. But it is by no means certain how bold the new left, splintered and still facing a strong challenge from the entrenched right, is going to be. Whether the left is able to assert itself in the ideological battle with the right remains to be seen.

Chapter Five:

Human Rights and the Rule of Law

At Long Last Someone Takes A Stand

June 25, 2008

Britain is in the midst of an extraordinary national debate on civil liberties. It comes after the decision by a leading member of the opposition Conservative Party to resign his seat in Parliament and stand again in a by-election over the single issue of the erosion of civil liberties. The politician, David Davis, made the announcement in the wake of a decision in the British House of Commons to extend detention of any individual for up to 42 days without being charged under antiterrorism laws. It comes amid mounting opposition to the use of anti-terror laws for a wide variety of offenses, including, in some cases, minor transgressions attracting financial penalties imposed by local councils.

Britain's Liberal Democratic Party, which came second in Davis's constituency last time, has said it will not put up a candidate against him in the by-election expected to take place next month. Even some prominent politicians of the governing Labour Party have announced that they will support Davis, despite threats that they will be expelled from the party. The volume of e-mail and other messages of support is extraordinary. Anti-terror laws, their use seen as arbitrary and widespread, are beginning to backfire.

Prime Minister Gordon Brown takes comfort in pointing out that two-thirds of the British people in a recent survey supported the extension of detention without trial for up to 42 days—in effect, suspension of the right to habeas corpus for a period nearly equivalent to a three-month prison sentence in the United Kingdom. Supporters of Davis's move say that if the British people really believe on reflection that that is what they want, then they should exercise their right to decide whether he should continue as their MP. At the very least, his resignation gives an opportunity for that reflection. Otherwise, the matter would be left to the House of Lords and courts. They are certainly among the guardians of our liberties, but it is essential that the citizen, too, remains involved in this debate.

The 2007 annual report of Amnesty International on the state of human rights worldwide says, "Powerful governments and armed groups are deliberately fomenting fear to erode human rights and to create an increasingly polarized and dangerous world." The message of Amnesty reflects something that has become increasingly obvious since 9/11. The "war on terror" has left a long trail of human rights abuses and created deep divisions that cast a shadow on international relations, making the world more dangerous. In one of the strongest repudiations of the policies of Western governments, the secretary-general of Amnesty, Irene Khan, said, "The politics of fear are fuelling a downward spiral of human rights abuses in which no right is sacrosanct and no person safe." She accused governments of adopting policies which undermine the rule of law, feed racism and xenophobia, divide communities, intensify inequalities and sow the seeds for more violence and conflict.

Old-fashioned repression has gained a new lease of life under the guise of fighting terrorism in some countries, while in others, including the United Kingdom, loosely defined counter-terrorism laws pose a threat to civil liberties, including free speech. Among the leaders named by Amnesty International for playing on fear among their supporters to help them push their own political agendas and strengthen their political power are President George W. Bush, now ex-Prime Minister John Howard of Australia, President Omar al-Bashir of Sudan and President Robert Mugabe of Zimbabwe. Nothing can be more serious than when leading countries of the free world find themselves in the same league as the most barbaric when it comes to human rights.

The 2008 report of Human Rights Watch mourns the state of democracy with these words: "Rarely has democracy been so acclaimed, yet so breached, so promoted yet so disrespected, so important yet so disappointing." From Pakistan, China and Russia to Uzbekistan, Egypt, Ethiopia and Zimbabwe, every dictator or totalitarian regime aspires to the status conferred by the label of democracy. They all used repression before. The rhetoric which President George W. Bush has introduced since the beginning of his "war on terror" and crusade for "democracy" have given such regimes a new lease on life. Human

Rights Watch accuses the Bush administration of embracing this route instead of defending human rights, because talk of human rights leads to Guantanamo, secret CIA prisons abroad, simulated drowning and other forms of "rendition," military commissions and the suspension of habeas corpus. Amnesty and Human Rights Watch are two of the world's leading organizations in the field of human rights. How did they reach conclusions so bleak?

The dawn of the twenty-first century bears a strange resemblance to the circumstances that led to the grant of Magna Carta in 1215. In the early thirteenth century, King John of England had invaded France and, in the ensuing wars, had captured large pieces of territory in the west. By 1214, he had stretched his military too far and was defeated in the battle of Bouvines near Lille in that year. They were disastrous wars and the costs in terms of lives lost and money needed to finance them unsustainable. The king's income from the occupied land in France had dried up. The king demanded higher payments from his barons to make up for the deficit and more individuals to serve as knights in his military. He did not have much sympathy for his subjects. He appointed all of England's county judges, who imposed harsh penalties on dissenters, seizing their properties and possessions in many cases.

In 1215, King John was unpopular. His policies in fighting ruinous wars and funding them through excessive coercion against his subjects generated resentment. At a time of economic difficulties, his proclamations to raise money and troops caused more hardship for the people of his kingdom. There was a rebellion led by some of the most important barons, who complained that the king's demands had become unreasonable, breaking all rules of customary fairness. They were supported by the city of London and others not in open revolt. King John's authority had already suffered in previous defeats and because of a bitter dispute with the pope over election of the archbishop of Canterbury. The growing rebellion at home posed a grave threat to his crown.

In an attempt to avoid a civil war, King John put his seal on two documents of concessions in June 1215. One was Magna Carta, the Great Charter of Freedoms. The other, the Charter of the Forest, promised the subsistence rights to the poor. Although Magna Carta was not a bill of rights for the king's subjects, it had the opposite effect. Its principles remain the source of the most fundamental freedoms today for every individual. The right to habeas corpus, prohibition of torture, trial by jury and the rule of law all derive from Chapter 39 of the Great Charter of 1215, which says that no free man shall be arrested or imprisoned or victimized or attacked in any way, except by the judgment of his peers or by the law of the land. Habeas corpus is an extraordinary legal remedy. It empowers courts, even places a duty upon them, to command the state to produce a person whose liberty has been taken away and show cause why. It is the ultimate safeguard against unlawful detention and is written in the American constitution, English law and all its derivatives throughout the world. That right is at stake here as the nation reflects on the extension of suspension of habeas corpus for as long as 42 days.

An adage used today by legal experts stresses that "justice delayed is justice denied." It is the basis for an individual's right to be produced in court without delay and to a speedy trial once charged. Or it would be unfair to the injured party, who must be presumed innocent until proven guilty. The promise can be traced back to Chapter 40 of Magna Carta, in which King John agreed: "To no one will we sell, to no one deny or delay right or justice."

A growing number of people in Britain are beginning to say these guarantees are at stake today. Questions are being asked where is this taking the country? Should a weak and tired government be allowed to get away with restricting the most fundamental freedoms when a large body of stalwarts—politicians, legal experts, law-enforcement officers and enlightened citizens—cannot be persuaded? Should a narrow victory in Parliament by nine votes (315-306), made possible by coercion and enticements, not make people think that more reflection and deliberation are needed on this matter, both inside and outside the House of Lords? If what the government can point to is one public opinion survey to justify curtailing the most fundamental right in a democratic society, then where does it lead to? Is the majority, indicated in opinion surveys, at any given point sufficient to target a particular community or to bring back hanging that much of the civilized world, except for America, shuns?

Such scenarios may seem democratic to some, but opponents argue that they quickly destroy democracy. To them, democracy is not just an abstract idea. It is about how people live in a free society. This is a debate that is likely to continue in the United Kingdom well after President George W. Bush leaves the White House in January 2009.

Uproar in "Police State" Britain

November 28, 2008

The arrest and interrogation of Damian Green, one of Britain's leading opposition politicians, by the counterterrorism police on November 27, 2008 on "suspicion of conspiring to commit misconduct in a public office" is an extraordinary event. Counterterrorism officers searched his homes and offices in London and his constituency. He was questioned for nine hours and released on bail without charge, but must return next February for further questioning. The police action happened when the world's attention was focused on the terrorist attacks in the Indian city of Mumbai.

The Conservative Party, main opposition in the British Parliament that has been leading in opinion polls this year, is furious at the treatment of one of its star performers. In all probability, Green, a former journalist on the Times of London, would be a minister if the Conservatives won the next general election. He had raised some uncomfortable questions for Prime Minister Gordon Brown and his government in the past year. In November 2007, he disclosed that the home secretary knew as many as 5,000 illegal immigrants had been granted licenses to work by the Security Industry Authority, but decided not to make the information public.

In February, Damian Green revealed that an illegal immigrant had been employed as a cleaner in the British Parliament and raised questions over its security implications. Then, there was a letter from the home secretary warning that a recession could lead to an increase in crime. He confronted the British government at a time when public concern over crime was rising. The Home Office later admitted that serious crime had been underestimated in official statistics. Green further made public the existence of a list of Labour MPs who could rebel against their own government's draft legislation to extend the period of detention without charge to 42 days.

I have already mentioned that the arrest and interrogation of Damian Green came on "suspicion of conspiring to commit misconduct in a public office." This seems to be related to information passed on to him by a whistleblower in the Home Office—an official who saw government wrongdoing and brought it to the attention of a leading opposition MP. The episode has fuelled worries over the loosely-worded anti-terror laws pushed after September 11, 2001 by Tony Blair, the previous prime minister, and their misuse to suppress information likely to embarrass the government.

A number of senior political figures were informed about the Conservative shadow minister's arrest shortly before it happened. Among them were the Conservative leader David Cameron, the London Mayor who is responsible for running the Metropolitan Police Force and the Speaker of the British House of Commons. The Home Secretary and others in the government have flatly denied prior knowledge of the arrest. However, an ex-Home Secretary, Kenneth Clarke, says he cannot believe that ministers did not know in advance what was about to happen.

Reports and comments on how a prominent politician has been treated under anti-terror laws are all over the British press today. The London Mayor expressed his "trenchant concerns" when told of the impending arrest. David Davies, former shadow home secretary who resigned in protest at the threat to civil liberties earlier this year, has called the situation "reminiscent to Robert Mugabe's Zimbabwe." The Conservative leader David Cameron has described the action as "Stalinesque" and said the ministers have some serious questions to answer. "If the police wanted answers from him, why did they not pick up the phone," Cameron asked.

The timing and possible motives of what has happened are worth considering. Politicians, especially those in power, are very good at engaging in questionable acts when there are bigger events taking place elsewhere. Damian Green's arrest and interrogation happened when the British public was focused on the terrorist attacks in India—attacks in which there had been hundreds of casualties, including British. There were already numerous examples where anti-terror laws had been used against people who had nothing to do with terror. Journalists and researchers are under unprecedented pressure. Academics at British universities have all but resigned themselves because of the shifting and arbitrary interpretations by the authorities of the meaning and causes of terrorism, to save their careers and to ensure funding for their projects. The picture is bleak and shows that when governments are able to seize too much power, they abuse it to the detriment of citizens.

Was the arrest of one of Britain's leading politicians, possibly a future minister, aimed at sending a message to lesser people in the country to close their eyes, ears and mouths? The good news is that criticism of the police action has been swift, widespread and strong and has only begun. As a front-bench member of the British Parliament, Damian Green has "parliamentary privileges" which would be hard to challenge. His actions are in the public interest. For this reason alone, the government would be foolish to prosecute him in court. Green says it is his job as an opposition politician to hold the government to account, and he has every intention of continuing to do so.

MASSACRE IN LAHORE

May 29, 2010

Even for a country where violence has long become routine, the orgy of killing in Pakistan at Friday's prayers in Lahore is particularly distressing. Men armed with guns, hand grenades, wearing suicide vests, killed nearly 80 people and wounded more than 100 at Garhi Shahu and Model Town in the capital of Pakistan's Punjab province. Three suicide bombers blew themselves up as security forces began closing in.

It is important to say a few words here about the victims. They were members of the Ahmadiyya sect of Muslims, regarded as heretics by many other Muslims, particularly hardline Sunnis. Pakistan has a four million-strong Ahmadiyya community, officially regarded as non-Muslims. They have long been persecuted and the discrimination against them continues to date. In 1984, Pakistan's military dictator General Ziaul Haq issued an edict that prohibited Ahmadis to call themselves Muslim or "to pose as Muslims." General Zia then enjoyed the patronage of the United States president Ronald Reagan. At the time, Washington was providing Zia with billions of dollars of military and economic aid, and arming and encouraging Sunni Islamic fundamentalism, to fight Soviet communism in Afghanistan.

Ahmadis, in fact, claim to lead the revival of peaceful propagation of Islam. The sect's founder Ghulam Ahmad (1835—1908) proclaimed himself to be the Mujahid (divine reformer) of the fourteenth Islamic century. Among the most objectionable aspects of Ahmadiyya beliefs is their view on the death and return of Jesus. The massacre on Friday at Ahmadiyya mosques in Lahore is yet another reminder of the folly of feeding bigotry and intolerance that always leads to unforeseen disastrous consequences. The same fundamentalists the Americans fed, and their children, confront their erstwhile masters today. They kill fellow citizens who do not conform to their interpretation of Islam, as well as those who do.

DRONE WARS: HOW MANY MORE?

October 29, 2012

Now we know that not only did the United Kingdom already have drones, but more are coming to join the Royal Air Force for surveillance and combat operations in foreign lands. And, for the first time, they will be controlled from Britain. According to a report in the Guardian, the United Kingdom has made urgent purchase of five more Reaper unmanned aerial vehicles, which will double their number with the British military. Initially, they will be deployed in Afghanistan and are expected to start operating within weeks. So, instead of sitting with their American counterparts in Nevada, the British "pilots" will be playing with videogame killing machines from RAF Waddington in the English county of Lincolnshire. These latest developments come as the United Nations has finally decided to investigate American drone strikes and other "targeted killings" of terrorist suspects.

In the main, three factors have influenced the British government's decision: the prolongation of the war in Afghanistan beyond the military planners' original estimates; the rise in the deaths and injuries of British and other NATO soldiers at the hands of Afghan security personnel; and President Obama's plan to withdraw most of the U.S. combat troops from Afghanistan by the end of 2014. Surely other NATO troops cannot stay in the country beyond that point.

Whether President Obama is reelected or Mitt Romney wins on November 6, it can be taken as certain that drone wars will continue in Pakistan, Afghanistan, Yemen and their use will be extended to other places. So mechanized, refined and cheap to manufacture are these instruments of the "war on terror." In the present economic difficulties, the governing coalition of Conservative prime minister David Cameron and his Liberal-Democrat deputy Nick Clegg probably feels that Britain's urgent purchase of Reaper drones is a "good investment."

Sources in touch with American policymakers in Washington confidently predict that drone wars will continue. So, there seems to be no reason for the British government to withdraw its aircraft from the region. Under rules imposed by the European Union and the Civil Aviation Authority, drone missions can only be flown in certain places in Britain. In a recent article, I discussed a study by Stanford and New York universities' law schools. It concluded that the CIA's targeted drone killings in Pakistan's tribal areas were politically counterproductive, killing many civilians and undermining respect for international law.

That British drones have been in operation from Creech air base in the United States has been a less known fact. The Ministry of Defence in London insists that only four civilians have died in its drone operations in Afghanistan—in line with the Obama administration's claims of there being very few civilian casualties. However, British defence officials say they have no idea how many insurgents have died because of the "immense difficulty and risks" of verifying who has been hit.

Clive Stafford Smith, founder of the legal charity Reprieve, says that "decisions are being made that will ripple through the generations." In a recent comment, he wrote: "Just as the secret Manhattan Project ushered in the nuclear age, so the military and their corporate colleagues are pressing forward with policies with very little public disclosure or debate." It is wholly inconsistent for any Western leader or government to assert that they have no idea how many insurgents have died because of "immense difficulty and risks" and yet for Prime Minister David Cameron to claim that by December 2010 British drones had "killed 124 insurgents in Afghanistan." No wonder defence officials denied that the information came from them, and said that "they had no idea where the prime minister got the figure." So the question arises, as Smith has raised, whether the kill-numbers are being "conjured up by politicians."

For several years since the "war on terror" started a decade ago, the British government has sought to deny accusations that its forces have been involved in terror and torture—against mounting evidence. The Stanford and New York universities' report is among the latest and most damning. The truth about the use of circling drones to terrify the 800,000 citizens—men, women and children—in a remote tribal region is a kind of war forbidden under the Geneva conventions. But the rules of war are being changed with disregard for established conventions and law. The West's drone policy is on trial.

In a legal challenge before the High Court in London brought by a man who lost his father in a CIA drone strike, Britain once again faces accusations of providing intelligence for such attacks and therefore of complicity. After reading a harrowing account of drone terror from Noor Khan, a resident of northwestern Pakistan, Lord Justice Moses described the evidence as "very moving." It is our responsibility as citizens wherever we may be to read Noor Khan's testimony and ask ourselves, "How many more?"

ASSANGE, PINOCHET AND DIPLOMATIC
DOUBLE-DEALING

August 24, 2012

A decade ago, the British government of Labour prime minister Tony
Blair decided to back President George W. Bush's decision to invade Iraq
even though foreign office lawyers in London had warned that such an
attack had no "legal basis in international law." In the midst of sharp
divisions in government and British society, the invasion went ahead
in March 2003. The consequences were far-reaching and they undermined the Blair government's authority at home. Limping thereafter, he
resigned in June 2007, humbled and apologetic. War and the economy
together played no mean part in Tony Blair's fall in British politics and
the Labour Party's defeat three years later.

A few days ago, Britain's Foreign Secretary William Hague person-
ally approved a letter which was sent to Ecuador. Its details were taken
as a threat to raid the Ecuadorean Embassy in London and drag out
WikiLeaks' founder Julian Assange for extradition to Sweden, where
state prosecutors say they want to question him about complaints of
sexual assault. Hague's letter was delivered to Ecuador despite the "grave
reservations of lawyers in his department." Speaking anonymously to the
Independent newspaper, a senior British official said that "staff feared
the move could provoke retaliatory attacks against British embassies
overseas." A large majority in the Organization of American States
is up in arms. Outside the Americas too, Britain is struggling to find
much sympathy for its stance. In soccer parlance, Prime Minister David
Cameron's center forward has scored a spectacular own goal.

While Julian Assange made a statement from the balcony of the Ecua-
dorean Embassy in London, attacking America's "witch hunt" against
WikiLeaks and journalistic freedom, several former mandarins of the
British Diplomatic Service expressed serious misgivings over William

Hague's handling of the affair. Oliver Miles, a 40-year veteran, described the letter to Ecuador as a "big mistake," because "it puts the British government in the position of asking for something illegitimate." Former ambassador to Moscow, Tony Brenton, commented that the Foreign Office had "slightly overreached themselves, for both legal and practical reasons." And a former envoy to Uzbekistan, Craig Murray, said, "You cannot simply legislate domestically and opt out of international law."

Otherwise, the mainstream broadcast and print media continued to provide a running commentary of the whole affair. The coverage has been generally confused, selective, repetitive and often hostile to Assange and a small Latin American country's decision to grant him asylum. The Economist, though, positioning itself on the other side, criticized Britain's "ham-handed invocation of a never-used, 1987 law to insinuate that it could, eventually, have the right to enter the embassy."

It is perhaps necessary at this point to take note of the London-based Bertha Foundation's legal director Jennifer Robinson, who has described the British Foreign Office's letter and the implicit threat as unprecedented—one which, if implemented, would force a profound change in the conduct of international diplomacy. Also important is to take a look at the concerns raised by prominent American feminist writer Naomi Wolf in an article titled "Something Rotten in the State of Sweden: 8 Big Problems with the 'Case' Against Assange." Under her microscope is the entire Swedish legal system.

Why does Assange and others fear that Sweden would extradite him to the United States, where he could face the rest of his life in jail, even execution for publishing leaked official documents? Because in November 2006 the United Nations found Sweden guilty of violating the global torture ban. Swedish officials handed over Mohammed El Zari and Ahmed Agiza, two Egyptian asylum seekers, to CIA operatives in December 2001, to be rendered from Stockholm to Cairo. Both were tortured in Egypt. And, as Seamus Milne wrote in the Guardian, because of reports of a secret indictment against Assange by a U.S. federal grand jury in Alexandria, Virginia.

The law says that someone who has suffered persecution, or fears that he or she will suffer persecution because of race, religion, nationality, membership of a particular group or political opinion may seek asylum.

In the last few days, the United States has claimed that it does not recognize the concept of "diplomatic asylum." Exactly what distinction is Washington trying to make between asylum, political asylum and diplomatic asylum is baffling. Assange was after all in the territory of a foreign country that granted him refuge. Let us look at some precedents.

Stalin's daughter Svetlana sought asylum when she walked into the U.S. Embassy in Delhi in 1967. Aleksandr Solzhenitsyn got asylum and lived in the United States for years before returning to Russia. Martina Navratilova, the Czech tennis player, took asylum in the U.S. in 1975. There are numerous instances when dissidents have been granted refuge in the United States and elsewhere. The concept is universal and depends on the sovereign decision of the country dealing with an asylum request.

Also worth examining is the British foreign secretary's assertion that the United Kingdom has a "binding obligation" to extradite Assange to Sweden. Let us, for a moment, go back to October 1998. Chile's former military dictator Augusto Pinochet was visiting London for medical treatment. A Spanish magistrate Baltasar Garzon, now on Assange's legal team, issued an arrest warrant for Pinochet on charges arising out of crimes against humanity in Chile. Pinochet was arrested a few days later in Britain, where he would spend more than a year in judicial custody, fighting extradition to Spain. The House of Lords, then Britain's highest court, ruled that Pinochet could indeed be handed over to the Spanish judicial authorities, because crimes such as torture could not be protected by immunity.

The British government nonetheless allowed Pinochet to return to Chile in March 2000 on health grounds. The law was clear, but for Britain's Labour government at the time there was no "binding obligation" to extradite Pinochet to Spain. Chile under Pinochet had backed the United Kingdom during the brief Falklands war with Argentina. Moreover, he and Britain's former Conservative prime minister Margaret Thatcher were admirers of each other. There was, after all, a way out for Pinochet to return home instead of being extradited to Spain.

Writing about the essence of rule of law and government's legitimacy, Thomas Hobbes in his seventeenth-century work Leviathan observed: "The law is the public conscience." What conscience?

Chapter Six:

War On Terror

A New Age Of Torture

August 19, 2008

The appearance of Dr. Aafia Siddiqui in a New York court on August 5 has brought another disturbing episode in the "war on terror" of President George W. Bush to light. According to a lawyer acting for Dr. Siddiqui, an American-educated scientist of Pakistani origin, her client was brought to New York after spending several years in U.S. custody at an unknown place, thought to be the Bagram air base in Afghanistan. While in detention, she suffered "horrendous physical and psychological torture." The American authorities claimed that they captured Dr. Siddiqui only in July 2008, accusing her of attacking U.S. military officers and being an al Qaeda operative. These charges have been dismissed by the Human Rights Commission of Pakistan.

The case has drawn international attention, coming at a time when the Bush administration, in its last few months, appears determined to put as many detainees captured during its "war on terror" as possible on trial. According to Dr. Siddiqui's lawyer, New York has been chosen as the venue for her trial because it is the city of Twin Towers, where the sentiment is likely to be most prejudicial and the November elections are close. Just before Dr. Siddiqui was produced in court in New York, a U.S. military commission in the Guantanamo Bay detention camp convicted and sentenced Salim Hamdan, Osama bin Laden's driver, to five-and-a-half years in prison. Amnesty International and Human Rights Watch both criticized the Guantanamo trial as falling below the acceptable standards of justice.

Aleksandr Solzhenitsyn describes in the opening chapter named "Arrest" in The Gulag Archipelago how it feels when someone is seized by shadowy individuals, about whom the victim knows nothing and has no clue as to what lies ahead. Solzhenitsyn wrote: "Arrest! Need it be said that it is a breaking point in your life. A bolt of lightning which has scored a direct hit on you." On September 6, 2006, President George W.

Bush admitted the existence of a secret CIA program to abduct, detain and interrogate people outside America as part of his "war on terror." In a statement intended to portray himself as a strong leader, Bush referred to the CIA interrogation techniques as tough, lawful and necessary. His message, which gave few insights, was that "we are getting vital information necessary to do our jobs and that is to protect the American people and our allies." The President said he could not describe the methods used, but wanted everyone to understand why. The admission followed months of media reports in America and Europe and protests by nongovernmental organizations that had made the administration's continued silence untenable.

Why did the U.S. administration choose to operate secret prisons abroad? Where were they located and what kind of interrogation techniques were in use there to get what Bush described glibly as vital information? Glossy assertions, in the guise of confidentiality, became the hallmark of the Bush administration as the "war on terror" progressed. The official justification became that "we in the civilized world face an unparalleled and escalating terrorist threat and extraordinary measures are required" to deal with it. The administration knows it all. The people should simply believe what they are told, although the lesson of history is that laws are invariably broken when there is unwarranted secrecy and appropriate constitutional supervision is absent. Where the Bush administration led, other governments followed. From Britain, Italy and Australia to Russia, China and elsewhere, talk of the terrorist threat became engrained in government polemics. Among the most disturbing aspects was the Chinese leadership's description of protests by Buddhist monks in Tibet as terrorist activity.

Reports, which first surfaced in 2005, of secret CIA prisons in European and other locations were confirmed in an investigation by the Council of Europe in June 2007. The investigation, conducted by the Swiss Senator, Dick Marty, concluded that "large numbers of people had been abducted across the world" and transferred to countries where "torture is common practice." Others were kept in "arbitrary detention without any precise charge" and without any judicial oversight. Still others had "disappeared for indefinite periods, held in secret prisons, including in member-states of the Council of Europe, the existence and operation of which had been concealed."

Dick Marty said in his report that these people were subjected to degrading treatment and torture to extract information, however unsound, which America claimed "had protected our common security." Prisoners were interrogated ceaselessly and physically and psychologically abused before being released because they were "plainly not the people being sought." The report said that these were the terrible consequences of what in some quarters is called the "war on terror." The report specifically named Romania and Poland, where the CIA ran secret prisons and torture centers.

How were prisoners taken to such camps and what was done to them? It turned out that the CIA first abducted people, including children as young as seven, across the world. The agency was then able to fly captives, under an agreement by all NATO members, including Britain, which granted blanket over-flight clearances to American and allied forces involved in the fight against terrorism. Apart from Poland and Romania, former Soviet bloc countries where successors of the dreaded Communist intelligence services operated, Chechnya, the former Yugoslav Republic of Macedonia and Syria were among other destinations named, as well as Italy, where abductions by the CIA took place. The report said that the systematic exporting of torture outside the United States and the reservation of such methods exclusively for non-Americans amounted to an "apartheid" mentality, which fuels anti-Americanism and creates sympathy for Islamic fundamentalism.

What went on inside the Abu Ghraib prison in Iraq is truly horrific, with thousands of men, women and children kept there at a time. Pouring acid on captives, forcing them to remove their clothing, keeping them naked for days in low temperatures and pouring cold water on them, arranging naked male prisoners in a pile and jumping on them, forcing them to wear women's underwear, taking photographs of dead prisoners and threatening captives with rape—such "blatant, sadistic and wanton" abuses of Iraqis were carried out by American soldiers in the prison. All this and more was done to them when, in many cases, their jailers did not even know their identities or the reasons for their detention.

Other examples of the culture of torture are recorded in numerous pictures of Abu Ghraib abuses now in the public domain. A young American soldier, Sabrina Harman, took many of these pictures during her tour of duty inside the prison. Like so many other young American soldiers, she joined the military to help pay for her college education. In March 2008, The New Yorker published her story with photos she took of abuses committed on prisoners. The pictures provided a graphic illustration of the abuses which America itself admitted in the official Taguba Report. The inquiry resulted in a number of largely low-ranking reservists who either took the pictures, or were seen in them, portrayed as "rogues who acted out of depravity." Documents obtained by the Washington Post and the American Civil Liberties Union showed that the senior military officer in Iraq, General Ricardo Sanchez, had actually authorized the use of military dogs, extreme temperatures, reverse sleep patterns and sensory deprivation as interrogation techniques in Abu Ghraib.

As The New Yorker said, Abu Ghraib was "de facto United States policy." And the "authorization and decriminalization of cruel, inhuman and degrading treatment of captives in wartime have been among the defining legacies" of the Bush administration. The techniques of interrogation were a direct result of the administration's hostility to international law—the doctrine of extracting confessions by torture flowing from the White House, the Vice President's office and a small number of senior Pentagon and Justice Department officials who had turned themselves into an oligarchy.

A new dawn comes with new hopes, but the dawn of the twenty-first century will forever be known for vengeance and brutal conflict for domination of energy resources in the Middle East. The attacks on September 11, 2001 were a wakeup call about the existing and future dangers. They were also a reminder of mistakes of the past. These mistakes were made in the final decade of the Cold War, the 1980s, when America's decision to favor extremist, against moderate, Islam in the region fanned the fires of hatred. In the decade after the Cold War, the 1990s, the battleground in Afghanistan was abandoned with the fires still burning.

Such mistakes created a sanctuary for the Taliban and al Qaeda. Far from learning the obvious lesson, the neoconservatives had a new agenda for the coming century, well before the events of 9/11. Globalization had gone too far. Economic and political power had rapidly begun to shift to Asia. The scope and intensity of the American project under the presidency of George W. Bush was an expression of the determination to draw back the center of gravity towards the West, with little realization that such course of action involved great risks.

POLICY TURN IN THE "WAR ON TERROR"

September 16, 2008

As George W. Bush limps towards the finish line of his turbulent presidency, two recent events on the other side of the globe, in the region that has been the main battleground in his "war on terror," are of particular interest. One, the ascendency of Asif Ali Zardari, the widower of Benazir Bhutto, to the presidency of Pakistan. The other, the decision by the 45-member Nuclear Suppliers' Group to grant a "waiver" to India, after intense lobbying by the White House. The "waiver" clears the way for India, a nuclear weapons state, to buy nuclear components and fuel for use in its civilian power plants. The interest of the Bush administration in this whole process has been strong and is indicative of America's changing policy in South Asia—be tougher with Pakistan and court India.

Under a unique arrangement, the International Atomic Energy Agency, the UN watchdog, and nuclear suppliers have agreed to do business with India. In doing so, they have accepted the reality of the country's nuclear arsenal. India refuses to sign the Western-backed Nuclear Non-Proliferation Treaty, arguing that the treaty is discriminatory against countries not recognized as nuclear powers. A separate agreement with the United States is yet to be approved by Congress. Only then will America be able to sell nuclear material and technology to India for civilian use. But India will soon be able to do business with other nuclear suppliers. An agreement with France is close.

The rise of Zardari to the presidency in Pakistan, and India's welcome into the nuclear club, may appear to be unconnected events, but are part of the same strategic environment in which the great powers, America and Russia, as well as emerging countries and regional players such as China, India and Pakistan, have to live. They are rivals, as well as allies. The long-term goal of each is to outdo the others economically and militarily, but they must cooperate in the short run as they pursue their objective.

There is a realization in Beijing, Delhi and Islamabad that the policy of the Bush administration has been too aggressive and militaristic. It exacerbated the phenomenon of terrorism which it professed to defeat. The toll in civilian deaths, injuries, broken families and exiled refugees is enormous. The anti-American sentiment has provided fuel to the fires of violence. It has created a serious threat to the stability of Pakistan and increasingly in parts of China and India. Recent bomb attacks in Delhi, killing and wounding scores of shoppers, are the latest sign of India's vulnerability to the growing militancy in the region. Even claims of the much-heralded American military surge and the resultant decline in the violence in Iraq should be seen in context.

Bob Woodward, the Washington Post's veteran reporter, speaks of a secret operation of targeted assassinations that has brought down violence in Iraq. I recently asked an Iraqi researcher, just back from Baghdad, after a meeting at a London think-tank what she thought was behind the reduction in violence. Her reply: "There is less killing because there is no one to kill in mixed Shi'a-Sunni communities. The unfortunate have already been killed. The fortunate have fled to safer places in Iraq, turning it into a deeply segregated society, or fled the country." Even so, civilian deaths in Iraq often go unnoticed in the international media while America boasts about a reduction in violence after the surge.

George W. Bush sits amid the vast wreckage left by his presidency. The two events I mentioned earlier—the election of Zardari in Pakistan and the entry of India into the nuclear club—have an important meaning for America's policy after Bush, irrespective of the result of the November 2008 election. The appetite for bloodthirsty militarism is diminished in the Bush White House. The simple-minded policy of reliance on Pakistan's military dictator, now ex-ruler General Pervez Musharraf, in the "war on terror" has failed. In the court of public opinion in the region and beyond, America stands in the dock. What can possibly be achieved in these circumstances with the same policies?

In Zardari as president, Pakistan has a leader that America can trust. He is controversial and weak. He needs to work with the military—something the Washington establishment prefers. The Pakistani military's need for American aid remains great. So, in the end, it is likely to listen to Washington, putting the history of hostility and distrust for the People's Party led by Zardari behind—for now.

The hope in Washington is that the coalition of Zardari, the civilian politician in the front, and the military can keep the rest of the Pakistani opposition at bay. The proclamation by President Zardari that he would fight the Islamist militants will go down well in Washington. However, with powerful agencies of Pakistan's military close to the fundamentalist groups which they have traditionally supported, there must remain doubts about his ability to deliver. The recent presidential directive, which allows the U.S. forces to launch attacks inside Pakistan from Afghanistan, has also begun to cause tensions with the Pakistani military. It cannot appear to be standing by as American military incursions take place, for fear of inflaming the public opinion in Pakistan even more.

America's new approach towards India, a secure democracy, is a recognition that the main bulwark against militancy cannot be Pakistan. It has to be Pakistan's rival, neighbor and the second most populous country after China. It marks the end of the traditional U.S. preference for Pakistan during the Cold War and again in the last seven years since 9/11. However, the rules of the game with India have to be different. India is too large and independent to be dictated to in the same way as Pakistan. Its economy is growing at a rapid rate. The west needs India as much as India needs the west. America's evolving policy is an acknowledgment of these realities. On one hand, with Pakistan facing escalating violence and disorder, the main frontier against turmoil is to be India. On the other, it would, in the long run, serve as a counter to the growing military and economic power of China.

Understanding Terror

October 18, 2008

The September 11, 2001 attacks on America and the "war on terror" prosecuted by President George W. Bush have brought the debate on terrorism into sharp focus. Hardly any country can claim to be immune from the threat of terrorism or the impact of the U.S. offensive worldwide. In Afghanistan, Iraq, and increasingly Pakistan, it means war. India, ex-Soviet republics in Central Asia and U.S. allies in the Gulf have become frontline states in the war against terrorism. Beyond the conflict zone, its manifestations can be seen in security operations. These include surveillance, kidnappings and detentions instigated by America and its allies, as well as immigration restrictions and checks on money transactions unprecedented in scale since the end of the Cold War.

When changes of such magnitude take place in the name of "war on terror," it is natural to ask what constitutes terror and what are its causes? The reluctance to confront these questions is far greater today than at any time in the last half century. "Terrorist" and "terrorism" have become widely used terms of abuse throughout the world by democratic and totalitarian regimes alike. Academics and human rights activists can be denied visas to enter the United State. The political opposition in Zimbabwe and Buddhist monks protesting against Chinese rule, even the Dalai Lama, are accused of engaging in terrorist activities.

There is no universally accepted definition of terrorism. The term is used so widely and for such a sweeping range of activities that anybody faces the risk of terrorism-related accusations. The absurdity of this approach has been demonstrated most recently by the British government's decision to use its counterterrorism laws to seize the UK-based assets of Icelandic companies following the collapse of an Icelandic bank, caught in the worldwide financial turmoil. The "terrorist" label is used primarily for non-state groups. States, with few exceptions, can employ extreme repressive measures without being called terrorist. The idea of citizens taking up arms against a repressive regime has been buried in history. It has been quite a turnaround since the 1970s and 1980s.

However, there is a way to understand the phenomenon of terrorism objectively, casting aside the subjectivity that clouds the debate. It is to examine terrorism through the microscope of "culture of violence." Conflicts such as those in Afghanistan, Iraq and Palestine serve as the reference points to study terrorism by this method.

Culture, as defined by E. B. Tylor, is "that complex whole which includes knowledge, belief, art, morals, law, customs and many other capabilities and habits acquired by ... [members] of society." Culture is the way of life which people follow in society without consciously thinking about how it came into being. It incorporates the impact of events, cultivated behavior, experience accumulated over time and social learning and is transmitted from generation to generation over years, decades, even centuries. The fundamental building block of a culture is trait. Traits assume many forms such as tools, houses and lifestyle. Culture represents patterns of behavior—family relationships, attitudes and acts towards neighbors and people from distant places. The way government encourages citizens to conform, or imposes sanctions on them, indicates a certain culture. It is a collective mentality involving shared ways of seeing, understanding and experiencing the world. It distinguishes the members of one group from another.

How does a culture of violence take root and how does it grow? The process can be seen in four, sometimes overlapping, phases, starting with internal conflict. In Afghanistan, it began with the fall of the monarchy in 1973 and conflict between rival forces in the country. Iraq had been a tightly controlled dictatorship under Saddam Hussein. Its history under Ba'athist rule, which ended with Saddam's overthrow in 2003, shows conflict within the ruling party and between the regime and opposition groups. The conflict in Palestine goes back at least to the First World War in the early twentieth century. It, too, can be described as an internal conflict, between Jews and Palestinians, who have competing claims to the same land. But it would be wrong to see the Israel-Palestinian conflict solely as an internal matter now. It is central to the wider Middle East crisis, in which external powers are involved, and oil is key.

The second phase in the growth of a violent culture is associated with the involvement of outside players fueling internal conflict. The conditions which led to Afghanistan falling under Communist domination in the 1970s and the war since then have much to do with the actions of the ex-Soviet Union, America and regional powers such as Pakistan, Saudi Arabia, Iran and, to a lesser extent, China and India. After the failed attempt to annex Kuwait in the early 1990s, the Iraqi regime was seriously weakened by the imposition of UN sanctions and no-fly zones by America, Britain and, for a period, France, excluding Iraqi aircraft from flying over large parts of northern and southern Iraq. Following the 2003 U.S.-led invasion and the dismantling of the Ba'athist regime, many state and non-state players moved into Iraq, starting a vicious cycle of violence along with internal forces which had been unleashed.

The third phase in the growth of a culture of violence involves disintegration of the state structure, as the case of Iraq illustrates. The disintegration of the Afghan state in the 1980s and 1990s was a slow process. Once the institutions had collapsed, the Taliban were left as the only agency with the coercive power necessary to enforce some kind of order. The system which the Taliban imposed was oppressive and isolationist. It turned Afghanistan into a sanctuary for groups like al Qaeda.

The fourth stage is the creation of an environment in which the rise of extremism occurs. By this stage, the cycle of violence has matured; violence has superseded the rule of law; violent players and their victims have become used to coercion; and their thinking and behavior are driven by the perceived justification for, or expectation of, the use of force to resolve matters. In short, a condition has been reached in which violence permeates all levels of society and becomes part of human thinking, behavior and way of life. The reign of terror has arrived and becomes a phenomenon that does not know borders.

PAKISTAN IN CRISIS

May 6, 2009

President Asif Ali Zardari of Pakistan is on his first visit to the United States. His visit comes at a critical time for Pakistan and for America's relations with that nuclear-armed, but failing, country in South Asia. President Hamid Karzai of Afghanistan, Pakistan's failed neighbor, is also in Washington for trilateral meetings with President Obama and other leading figures in the administration.

Recent escalation of violence in Pakistan has brought grim warnings from senior American officials in Washington about the viability of the Pakistani state. A month ago, General David Petraeus, the top military commander in the region, testified in the Senate Armed Services Committee that "militant extremists could literally take down the Pakistani state" if left unchallenged. On the same day, a senior Pentagon official, Michele Flournoy, warned of higher U.S. casualties in Afghanistan in the coming year. And Admiral Eric Olson, chief of America's special operations commandos, described the situation in Afghanistan and Pakistan as "increasingly dire." According to one report, General Petraeus has privately told the White House that the administration has very little time to determine its future course of action in Pakistan as the civilian government of President Asif Ali Zardari struggles against an insurgency that is growing alarmingly.

For eight years under the Bush-Cheney presidency, the United States and its European allies were consumed in the fortification of the Western world following September 11, 2001. A vital part of this overwhelmingly militaristic approach was to remake West Asia, resulting in war and occupation in the region during the rest of the decade.

Amid all the media coverage of the threat to the West, what has often been missed is the eastward proliferation of terrorism, throughout Pakistan and to India and beyond. The Council for Foreign Relations, a New York-based research institution, while acknowledging the existence of "local terrorist groups" in the Indian part of the disputed region of Kashmir, goes on to say that "most of the recent terrorism has been conducted by Islamist outsiders who seek to claim Kashmir for Pakistan." According to the organization, many militants involved in attacks across the border in India received training in the same madrasahs where Taliban and al Qaeda fighters have studied since the 1980s. Some received training in Afghanistan when the Taliban ruled the country. Many more represent an indigenous phenomenon in Pakistani society.

With the advent of the 1990s, the rationale for arming militant Islamists to fight the Soviet Union had ceased. The Cold War had ended, the Soviet state had disintegrated and the Najibullah regime in Kabul had collapsed by 1992. The culture of violence had become embedded in Afghan and Pakistani societies. By the mid-1990s, the phenomenon of terrorism had mutated into something far more serious with the emergence of the Taliban, helped by Pakistan. After years of active intervention, the West had moved on to other priorities, leaving the Afghan chaos to its regional allies, Pakistan and Saudi Arabia.

It is true that there was not another 9/11-type attack on mainland America during the administration of George W. Bush. But this "success" must be seen in perspective. Historically, attacks by external forces on the United States are rare. Furthermore, the Oklahoma City bombing of 1995 and activities of anti-state private militias point to a domestic phenomenon in parts of America. Beyond the U.S. shores, the terrorist bombings in Madrid in 2004 and Bali and London a year later meant that the West continued to be targeted elsewhere. And thousands of U.S. and allied soldiers continued to die or be wounded in America's foreign wars.

In Pakistan, the conversion of local supporters of the Taliban to an indigenous group under the umbrella of Tehrik-i-Taliban Pakistan has been the most significant development responsible for the proliferation of violence. It began between 2002 and 2004 when Pakistan's armed forces were busy capturing "foreigners" to hand over to the Americans for money and carrying out military operations in areas linked to al Qaeda. Many of these operations were against groups in Balochistan and North-West Frontier Province, not allied to al Qaeda or the Taliban but against those demanding more autonomy and a greater share of income from local resources, principally Balochistan's gold, copper and coal mines and vast reserves of natural gas. Washington compensated the military regime of General Pervez Musharraf for prosecuting "anti-terrorism" operations inside Pakistan.

In such turbulent conditions, many local militant groups started to join ranks in Pakistan's frontier areas instead of merging into the Afghan Taliban. They developed their own distinct identity, sometimes launching attacks, at other times cutting deals with the authorities. According to the Council for Foreign Relations, the Taliban of Pakistan had become an effective fighting force of between 30,000 and 35,000 strong by 2008. They would network between themselves, as well as with the Afghan Taliban and al Qaeda when it suited them. Their aim—to oppose Pakistan's military and civilian government and to confront the U.S.-led forces in the region. The Pakistani Taliban have close affiliations with Jamiat ulema-i-Islam, a religious party which insists on the strict enforcement of Islamic law.

The leadership of Pakistan-based Kashmiri militants had connections with al Qaeda since before the advent of the Pakistani Taliban following the U.S. invasion of Afghanistan in late 2001. The leader of the Harakat-ul-Mujahideen group, Farooq Kashmiri Khalil, was a signatory to the 1998 declaration of war by al Qaeda. Quoting American and Indian officials, the Council for Foreign Relations said that Maulana Masood Azhar, leader of the Jaish-e-Muhammad group founded in 2000, is suspected of receiving money from al Qaeda. Another group, Lashkar-e-Taiba, has been active in the region since 1993.

Barely three months after 9/11, the Indian Parliament was attacked in December 2001. The Indian authorities accused Lashkar-e-Taiba and Jaish-e-Muhammad for the attack, in which more than a dozen people were killed, including all five attackers. A series of attacks followed. The most audacious was the three-day carnage in Mumbai, the main commercial city of India, in November 2008. There is plenty of evidence provided by experts and media reports in the United States, India, even Pakistan, that the attackers came from Pakistan. The group is said to have belonged to Lashkar-e-Taiba.

After vehement denials of Pakistani involvement in the Mumbai attack, Islamabad, against mounting evidence, admitted that the lone survivor among the gunmen, twenty-one-year-old Ajmal Kasab, was a Pakistani citizen.* As early as December 1, 2008, Britain's Guardian newspaper reported that he had been trained in marine warfare at a camp in Muzaffarabad in Pakistan-held Kashmir, part of a group of about 40 militants who had received commando training. The November 2008 carnage in Mumbai was the most high profile in a long sequence of attacks across India going back to the early 1990s.

The monster of terrorism in Pakistan is a consequence of policies followed over decades. At the heart of these policies has been a tendency to pursue high risk strategies, together with a state of denial. When the Pakistani state was established in 1947, the idea of a separate nation for the peoples of the Muslim faith of British India was not universally supported. Pashtuns under the leadership of Abdul Ghaffar Khan opposed partition. For years after the establishment of Pakistan, the Pashtuns and other minorities continued to challenge the domination of the most populous province, Punjab, in the country.

The response of Pakistan's ruling military-political elite has been suppression of the country's minorities. It happened in two ways: by coercive military methods and by playing the "Islamic card" in national politics. When minorities made demands for greater autonomy, they were portrayed as working against Islam and encountered military force. The fear of internal collapse is one of the main forces that determines the conduct of the military-political elite of Pakistan. The other is the perceived fear of India. Internal suppression at the expense of the rule of law and a national accord fuels resistance. Violence is diverted towards "external threats"—India on one side, Afghanistan on the other. For decades, this has been the essence of the high risk strategy of Pakistan's military-political establishment, especially its military intelligence organ, Inter-Services Intelligence Directorate.

The crisis for Pakistan has thus become the crisis for the entire region and beyond. Islamic fundamentalism encouraged by the military ruler, General Zia, to fight America's war in Afghanistan in the 1980s was devastatingly effective in defeating the Soviet Union and its client regime in Kabul. But the phenomenon undermined the rule of law and inflamed religious and sectarian violence. It has had a corrosive effect on national institutions. Pakistan is a failing state.

The election in November 2008 of Barack Obama was a revolutionary event. Obama's victory came with enormous odds and a strong desire for change. A leader who emerges in such conditions faces opposing demands. Like the end of the Vietnam era in the mid-1970s and the Cold War in the 1990s, the world's pre-eminent power looks for peace to recover and rebuild, but cannot make a hasty retreat. So the preference under the Obama presidency is to work for the beginning of the end of war and to switch to tough diplomacy. The task is turning out to be a lot harder than had been thought.

[*Ajmal Kasab was executed after trial by India in November 2012.]

EXCEPT KILLINGS, U.S. POLICY IS ACHIEVING LITTLE ELSE

April 6, 2010

Militants armed with guns, grenades and suicide car bombs attacked the American consulate and a political rally in Pakistan's North-West Frontier Province, killing nearly 50 people and wounding many more. The attacks were launched within minutes and were the most serious this year in Pakistan. These events raise serious questions about America's continuing military operations against Pashtun opposition in Afghanistan and Pakistan.

Pakistan's Taliban claimed responsibility for the consulate bombing in Peshawar, claiming it was in retaliation to America's drone war. The Taliban threatened further attacks on U.S. targets. The White House spokesman Robert Gibbs said the attack on the consulate was of "great concern" and that "we strongly condemn the violence." The first bomb of the day struck a political rally in the town of Timargarah in Lower Dir in the frontier region. According to an Awami National Party spokesman, members of the grouping had been celebrating plans to change the name of North-West Frontier Province when a suspected suicide bomber detonated his explosives.

Al Jazeera's Pakistan correspondent Kamal Hyder described the attack on the U.S. consulate in Peshawar as well coordinated. It shook the entire city, but did not cause the kind of mayhem seen in Dir. That will be the only consolation for the security agencies. These events underscore the fact that, despite American drone attacks, the Taliban remain a serious force. Al Jazeera correspondent suggested that although the militants had been driven out of their strongholds in key areas, a substantial number had infiltrated into the settled areas.

Meanwhile, a group of Afghan parliamentarians says that President Hamid Karzai, angry and frustrated at Washington and its allies criticizing and belittling his government, has threatened to step down and join the Taliban if foreign pressure on him continues. The Afghan MPs said it was the second time in recent days that Karzai had threatened to quit and join the Taliban. President Karzai has bitterly complained that he and his government are not sovereign and exercise little control over military operations.

Defying pressure from Washington to boycott Iran, the Indian government has decided to appoint its Tehran ambassador Sanjay Singh to represent the country at a two-day conference on nuclear disarmament in the Iranian capital beginning on April 17. Delhi also insisted that it had not shut its door on the pipeline project running from Iran through Pakistan to India. The Indian ambassador will attend the Tehran conference "Nuclear energy for All, Nuclear Weapons for None"—a sign of India's annoyance over constant diplomatic pressure from Washington that goes back to the Bush administration. Indian newspapers have quoted government sources in Delhi as saying that, as well as civilizational ties with Iran, Tehran is important for Delhi not just for energy, but also for strategic reasons in Afghanistan. The Tehran Times reported today the Indian envoy as saying that Iran can help India greatly in meeting its energy needs, including oil, gas and electricity.

India, Iran and Russia all cooperated in helping the Northern Alliance in the U.S.-led campaign to remove the Taliban, before President Bush turned against Iran in his 'axis of evil speech' in January 2002.

The Killing Of Osama Bin Laden

May 2, 2011

Ten years after the dreadful events of September 11, 2001, Osama bin Laden is dead. His killing in a CIA operation in the Pakistani colonial city of Abbottabad, about 30 miles from the capital, Islamabad, brings a closure for relatives of many thousands of victims of al Qaeda violence around the world. It will be seen as ultimate justice for the man viewed as the chief perpetrator of international terrorism for two decades. The sentiment is understandable, but there is a bigger truth. The 9/11 attacks on the World Trade Center and the Pentagon in the heart of America unleashed a global crisis. The subsequent "war on terror" so polarized the world that there will be those who will mourn bin Laden's death. It is an uncomfortable truth, but should not be overlooked. For although his physical presence may be behind us, the legend of Osama bin Laden still lives.

The biblical expression—Those who live by the sword will die by the sword—comes to mind. On the other side of the coin is the phrase—The enemy of my enemy is my friend. The simplicity and perils of this mindset are revealed by the manner of Osama bin Laden's death now and his creation at the outbreak of the CIA proxy war against the Soviet occupying forces in Afghanistan three decades ago. There is no dearth of experts associated with think tanks inside the Washington Beltway who claim with confidence that the United States had no contact with bin Laden, and did not help him. These claims are often based on the logic that bin Laden was already so hostile to the West that any warm relationship with the United States was out of the question. But Afghanistan's Mujahideen warlords were hostile to Western ideology as well. Their opposition was strengthened during the time they spent in the Arab world. Yet they and the West became allies in the war against the Soviet Union in Afghanistan.

Comments made by Britain's ex-foreign secretary Robin Cook in an article in the Guardian newspaper are worth noting at this point (The struggle against terrorism cannot be won by military means, July 8, 2005). In one passage, Cook, who had earlier resigned from Tony Blair's cabinet because of his opposition to the invasion of Iraq in 2003, said: "Bin Laden was ... a product of a monumental miscalculation by western security agencies. Throughout the 80s he was armed by the CIA and funded by the Saudis to wage jihad against the Russian occupation of Afghanistan. Al Qaeda, literally 'the database,' was originally the computer file of the thousands of mujahideen who were recruited and trained with help from the CIA to defeat the Russians. Inexplicably, and with disastrous consequences, it never appears to have occurred to Washington that once Russia was out of the way, Bin Laden's organization would turn its attention to the west."

Robin Cook was a politician of immense credibility. An ex-foreign secretary and leader of the House of Commons, another cabinet post, with access to classified information, his revelation after resigning would reasonably have to take precedence over other expert opinion. Cook did not live long after writing his article in the Guardian. He died unexpectedly of a heart attack barely a month later in August 2005. Had he lived, we may well have learned more from him. The purpose of my reference to the past is to make a point about the present. Hiring armed men driven by ideological zeal, and willing to fight your enemy for dollars, is a highway that goes through minefields, whether it is Afghanistan, Iraq, Libya or anywhere else.

The killing of bin Laden in a U.S. special forces operation will go a long way toward assuring the reelection of President Obama in November 2012. In the short run, though, the outcome has implications for al Qaeda, Pakistan and the West, including the United States. Bin Laden's demise has taken out America's most recognized and resourceful enemy, who inspired those discontented enough to kill innocent people. A wealthy man in his own right, he could both finance al Qaeda activities, and attract money from other sources. Many of those channels will surely be cut. But the risk of revenge attacks is real. The ruling establishment in Pakistan has to tread carefully. Already angry by frequent American drone attacks in the tribal areas, Pakistan's public opinion remains extremely sensitive to any U.S. military incursion so deep inside the country. Official reaction in Islamabad was therefore brief and non-committal.

Conflicting messages are coming from Washington and Islamabad about the degree of cooperation between the CIA and Pakistani military's Inter-Services Intelligence Directorate (ISI). Some sources claim that the Pakistani authorities had no idea about the American operation. President Obama, announcing that bin Laden had been targeted and killed by American forces, nevertheless said, "It is important to note that our counterterrorism cooperation with Pakistan helped us lead to bin Laden and the compound where he was hiding."

The episode raises many questions. Could it be true that Osama bin Laden had been living in an expensive home, especially built five years ago, next to the Pakistan Military Academy a few miles from the capital city, without the authorities having any clue? Would anything similar be possible close to West Point in the United States, Sandhurst in Britain or one of the military academies in India? Were there any Pakistanis who might have advised bin Laden to move from his hideout in Pakistan's northwestern tribal belt to a garrison town deep inside the country? If so, who were they?

The construction of a new mansion-style house in a colonial city is a big project and requires planning permission, preparation and supervision. In whose name was the application made? Who managed the building project so close to a premier military establishment? Was it all due to a series of monumental failures on many fronts? Or was there any involvement of Pakistan's security agencies, or individuals serving in them, and what may have been their motive? The whole episode is shrouded in mystery. Answers to some of these questions may come in time, but nothing is straightforward in the world of spies and clandestine operations.

There exists a difficult relationship between the United States and Pakistan's ISI, supposedly America's partner in the "war on terror" and simultaneously close to militant groups in Pakistan and Afghanistan. In reality, the ISI's past conduct shows that the agency has sometimes kept certain al Qaeda and Afghan Taliban figures from Washington, and handed others over to the CIA at other times. In a high-profile case, the arrest of Khalid Sheikh Mohammed, a leading al Qaeda figure, was announced in March 2003 from a "safe house" of a Pakistani military officer. The officer had family links with one of Pakistan's religious parties, Jamaat-i-Islami, which supported the military ruler General Pervez Musharraf, a close partner in President George W. Bush's war on terrorism.

In my book Overcoming the Bush Legacy in Iraq and Afghanistan, I have described how Sheikh Mohammed was protected and moved around by the ISI until he was handed over to the United States (Chapter 4, p 52). The conduct of Pakistani military and intelligence agencies in recent years suggests that while they have been willing to hand over "low-value" suspects or in many instances innocent people to the CIA, they have withheld the most valuable individuals. These people were passed on to the Americans when there was a likelihood of extracting a high price in return, or when the CIA confronted the Pakistani authorities with evidence that a wanted person was in Pakistan and the United States knew the location. Whether this was true in Osama bin Laden's case, or whether the recent controversy over the arrest of the CIA contractor Raymond Davis after the reported deaths of two Pakistani nationals in a firefight is relevant remains a topic of speculation.

The success of the operation to kill Osama bin Laden is certainly a major coup for President Obama—something his predecessor, George W. Bush did not manage in nearly eight years. It will boost Obama's popularity in the United States, and greatly improve his prospects in the November 2012 presidential election. However, it is unlikely to bring the threat of terrorism to an end, given the continuing conflicts in which the United States and allies are involved in the region. Since assuming the presidency more than two years ago, Obama has often repeated his intention to make sure that Osama bin Laden and al Qaeda are no longer a threat to America's security. The influence of al Qaeda seems to have declined in recent years, and the killing of bin Laden is the latest, most serious setback to the organization. Instead, the "Arab Spring" is sweeping across the region. While the peaceful mass movement demanding basic freedoms appears to have achieved some success in Egypt, the "Arab Spring" has to endure suppression in Bahrain, Jordan, Yemen and Syria. The conflict in Libya is more akin to tribal warfare, with Muammar Gaddafi's military apparently determined to crush the armed opposition which NATO supports. With bin Laden no longer on the scene, will President Obama seize the moment, refocus on the "Arab Spring" and let flowers bloom?

Just Plain Stupidity Or A Failure By Design

March 4, 2012

The explosion of national anger in Afghanistan after the revelation that U.S. soldiers dumped and burned copies of the Quran in an incineration pit has an uncanny familiarity with the history of previous foreign occupations of the country. Despite ceaseless official media campaign through the decade of U.S.-led war to convince us how well things were going for NATO, the battle for the hearts and minds in Afghanistan has not been won.

Dozens of Afghans have been killed in violent demonstrations across the country. Relations between foreign forces and civilians on one hand, and the Afghan population on the other, have sunk to a new low. The killings of two senior American military officers, deployed as "advisors" in the interior ministry, by an Afghan intelligence officer prompted NATO member-states to withdraw their "advisors" from all Afghan ministries and offices, for no one was deemed to be safe. Extraordinary scenes of public defiance looked so threatening that, in Washington, President Obama had to issue an apology. In Afghanistan, the U.S. commander Gen. John Allen apologized repeatedly and profusely.

There are those in Washington who will say it is easy for critics to deride the "achievements." The truth is that any military venture is ultimately judged by its final outcome. As President Obama prepares to end the Afghan venture launched by George W. Bush a decade ago, these events in early 2012 remind us of the chaos surrounding the 1989 Soviet military retreat. What will follow is anybody's guess, but the instinct of many in touch with Afghanistan will be to pray.

The burning of the Quran at Bagram Air Base, once a Soviet airfield when the Communist superpower occupied Afghanistan in the 1980s, was described by a BBC correspondent as NATO's tipping point in the country. The situation had been in the making almost from the beginning since the October 2001 invasion. The American military never understood that, in a country as impoverished but as rich in history and culture as Afghanistan, individual and national honor is the greatest asset. The failure to recognize this is particularly unfortunate for the United States, where so many politicians and those associated with the military-industrial complex would not stop talking about their honor and religious beliefs.

Is this failure down to the blindness of hubris? Or a disturbing level of prejudice against Muslims and Islam permeating certain sections of society and military? Is this the reckless instinct of a boyish mentality? Or a desperate method of finding a moment of laughter and entertainment in a highly stressful environment. Is it because of lack of training? Or no training is enough when irrationality rules human minds.

Acts such as the recent desecration of dead Afghan bodies by American marines urinating on them, and filming the episode, raise these awful but unavoidable questions. We have seen Abu Ghraib pictures of gross abuse of Iraqi prisoners before, and numerous other accounts are in the public domain. In Afghanistan, President Karzai has been vocal in his condemnation of such episodes as they occur with regular frequency. But apologies have become meaningless for most ordinary Afghans. It is difficult to think of anything more offensive than what was done to the dead bodies, and to the Quran, in a deeply religious country. Surely, professional soldiers from the United States, where religious roots are deep, should know better.

For more than a decade, the official version of the military intervention in Afghanistan focused on claims that the war aim was to defeat the Taliban, because first and foremost they were al Qaeda enablers and enemies of the Afghan people; that Western powers were friends and respecters of Islam and the Afghan population; that the United States would never again make the mistake of turning its back on Afghanistan as had happened in the early 1990s.

The credibility of each of these claims is seriously damaged today. The Obama administration is moving toward a withdrawal by the end of 2014. His military surge of 2009 has failed to overcome the Afghan resistance. And despite hearing many apologies, Afghans are not persuaded that foreign forces understand or respect their culture and sensitivities. The burning of the Quran was the last straw.

The consequences of the episode go beyond the withdrawal of American "advisors" from Afghan ministries and other government offices. Britain, France and Germany are among those NATO powers who have followed. Cooperation between the Afghan government, such as it was, and the international forces deployed there has become more strained. The BBC correspondent, Andrew North, reported there being "quiet fury" within the Afghan government with the Americans for their "brainless" behavior.

Other foreign military contingents are weary. The United Kingdom has signed a separate agreement with Kazakhstan, so British tanks and other military hardware can leave Afghanistan via Kazakh territory when UK troops withdraw. More deals with former Central Asian republics may be in the offing. And in a strange move given the reality of military balance in the country, the Americans have demanded that the Afghan government protect U.S. troops.

CHAPTER SEVEN:

EXCEPTIONALISM AND DEVIANCE

GAZA IN PERSPECTIVE

January 1, 2009

The bombing of the Gaza Strip has predictably been justified by Israel and the United States as self-defense by a country under attack from a "terrorist" organization. Claims of "surgical air attacks" against "carefully selected targets" to minimize civilian casualties, are repeated by Israeli politicians and government spokesmen in their daily encounters with the world media. In Jerusalem, as in Washington, the blame for the plight of Palestinians is placed entirely on Hamas, which rules the territory.

A little perspective is needed to understand what is really happening in Gaza. Roughly 400 Palestinians were killed and as many as 2,000 injured in the first five days of Israeli bombing until December 31, 2008. These casualties include children and young students, civilian officials and local policemen. The Gaza Strip is a small territory, about 140 square miles in area and a population of 1.5 million, making it one of the most densely populated places in the world. Israel, on the other hand, is a country of seven million people.

The scale of bloodshed in Gaza over five days is the same as if almost 2,000 Israelis had been killed and 9,000 wounded in the same period. Imagine the consequences for Israel in such an event. It begins to explain what the people of Gaza have already endured, and their horror is still not over. In contrast, the actual number of Israeli deaths by Hamas rockets fired randomly toward Israel recently is four.

Not only have Hamas security complexes and government buildings been hit. Mosques, schools, University buildings and civilian homes lie in ruins. Hospitals have been overwhelmed and shortages of medical supplies and food are making the situation increasingly desperate. Underground tunnels to Egypt, used to transport essential supplies as well as weapons and explosives, have been destroyed. Despite all this, the leader of Israel's Kadima Party, Foreign Minister Tzipi Livni, says the country has "no alternative" but to carry on.

The Israeli offensive was launched soon after the end of a six-month "ceasefire" with Hamas. In reality, no such ceasefire ever existed, because the continuing Israeli siege of Gaza amounts to an act of war. Richard Falk, the United Nations special rapporteur, has described the Israeli air attacks on the territory as "severe and massive violations of international law as defined in the Geneva Conventions, both in regard to the obligations of an occupying power and in the requirements of the laws of war." According to Professor Falk, Israel is guilty of inflicting collective punishment on the entire population of Gaza, of targeting civilians and of using disproportionate force, killing civilians and destroying the administrative infrastructure in the territory. Certainly, the Hamas rocket attacks against civilian targets in Israel are unlawful, he says. But that illegality does not give rise to any Israeli right to violate international humanitarian law and commit war crimes or crimes against humanity in response.

George W. Bush's Final Act:

A Bloody War In Gaza

January 9, 2009

George W. Bush was not going to leave the White House quietly. After eight days of relentless Israeli bombing of Gaza, he waved the green flag to Israel to invade the territory. In his weekly radio address, Bush held Hamas responsible for the latest violence, and proclaimed that "no peace deal would be acceptable without tougher action to prevent Hamas and other groups from receiving weapons." Hours later on January 3, Israeli tanks were rolling into the Gaza Strip. As the removals work in the White House, the conduct of George W. Bush in the last few days of his presidency shows that there is no change in him after eight years. He remains a hostage to his demons. His radio address is going to be remembered alongside television pictures of mutilated bodies of Palestinian children, beamed all over the world. The Bush presidency ends just as it began in 2001—with war.

A lot has happened in the intervening years, but the overpowering impression he leaves behind is that of a president who put political opportunism to most destructive use, wherever and however he could, to satisfy his own capriciousness and prejudices. With few exceptions, those in Congress in Washington and in other Western capitals simply caved in, because they did not want to be on the "wrong" side. The cost of this failure has been horrendous. As Bush prepares for quieter pastures in Texas, he leaves much of the Middle East and South Asia burning. Bush and his vice-president, Dick Cheney, have used every significant player that came in their path. From Tony Blair of Britain and General Pervez Musharraf of Pakistan to the Arab and East European countries, where abducted detainees were taken to be tortured, and to Mahmoud Abbas, president of the Palestinian Authority, and Israel's leading politicians—the list is long. As the end came near, the Bush-Cheney administration seized the opportunity offered by circumstances in and around Gaza.

A bitter dispute loomed in advance of January 8, when Abbas would complete his normal four-year term as Palestinian Authority president, having been elected in 2005. Hamas, the majority party in the Legislative Council, insisted that Abbas submit his resignation to the speaker and the process begin to hold a new presidential election. But Abbas was determined to hold on to power. His Fatah group argued that a law subsequently passed allowed him to remain in the post until the next council elections in 2010. As February elections approached in Israel, the Defense Minister and Labor Party leader, Ehud Barack, and the Foreign Minister and leader of the Kadima Party, Tzipi Livni, were in competition within the cabinet. The hardline Likud leader, Benjamin Netanyahu, goaded them from without. The leaders of Egypt and Jordan felt threatened by the emergence of Hamas and growing Iranian influence in the region. All this provided the ideal ground for Bush and Cheney to create a crisis and unleash the proxies on Gaza to reshape the territory. After Afghanistan and Iraq, it was the turn of Gaza to be subjected to "shock and awe." The command center for the operation is the White House, the proxies are in the region. The more insecure the proxies feel, the easier it is to play on their fears.

The events in Gaza bear echoes of the Sabra and Chatila massacres in Lebanon in September 1982. Then, Israel let loose its proxies, the Christian Phalange militiamen, on the two refugee camps. Hundreds of Palestinians—men, women and children—were killed and thousands injured. Now, Israeli bullets and bombs also kill women and children in Gaza, and the responsibility lies not in Tel Aviv, but in the White House. Despite all the talk of Hamas intransigence and its refusal to cease rocket attacks in Israel's border areas, truth does emerge from time to time.

Writing in the Huffington Post (Understanding the Gaza Catastrophe, January 3, 2009), the United Nations Special Rapporteur for Human Rights in the Palestinian Territories, Richard Falk, gives a detailed account of how the Hamas leadership "offered to extend the truce, even proposing a ten-year period." He writes, "Israel ignored these diplomatic initiatives and failed to carry out its side of the ceasefire agreement that involved some easing of the blockade that had been restricting the entry to Gaza of food, medicine and fuel to a trickle."

Cynical manipulation of fears and insecurities of others to punish peoples not liked in the White House has been the trademark of the Bush administration. His latest act is calculated to overthrow, or greatly weaken, Hamas in Gaza and, at the same time, to try to lock the path of the incoming administration of Barack Obama for the foreseeable future. Israel may finish its "military job" in Gaza in the next few weeks or months. Many more will die of bullets, lack of treatment, hunger and malnutrition. The rest will have to endure conditions worse than before. The sense of humiliation and betrayal will sink in deeper among Palestinians. The prospects of any diplomatic engagement with Hamas will have been set back. And America's image abroad takes another battering.

All of which would not matter to George W. Bush, for his green light to the Israelis to invade Gaza shows he has no remorse. An instinctive demolisher, he inspected the vast wreckage around him at the end of his presidency and decided to go with a bang—this time in Gaza. As the tragedy unfolds, Barack Obama's silence may seem odd, but he cannot be a happy man. Silence is the best signal to convey disengagement—if, indeed, it is that.

OBAMA'S PAKISTAN ENIGMA

April 7, 2009

A little over two months after assuming the United States presidency, Barack Obama is making waves in all directions. He leads at a time of multiple crises. The collapse of the economic and financial system, with worldwide consequences and a growing human cost, take center stage in the public discourse in America and Europe, but the threat of terrorism is not far behind. The West frets over the risk of another attack. A continent away in Afghanistan, Pakistan and, in recent days in Iraq, violence takes increasing numbers of lives every day. As Pakistan becomes the latest country to suffer a breakdown in order, new fears arise in the region and beyond. It is going to be a severe test of President Obama's evolving policy on the Afghan-Pakistan front.

The suicide bombing on a Shi'a mosque in Chakwal in the north of Punjab province two days ago seems to confirm a pattern in the escalating cycle of violence in Pakistan. About 20 people were blown up in the attack, including the suicide bomber, reported to be a boy dressed in black. Up to 100 were wounded. For some years, conventional wisdom had been that militant havens existed only in tribal areas along the Pakistan-Afghan frontier, and that attacks were launched on both sides from bases in the autonomous tribal belt. It is no longer the case.

The assassination of Pakistan's former Prime Minister, Benazir Bhutto, in Rawalpindi near Islamabad in December 2007 was a political earthquake. It laid bare the rapid proliferation of insurgency to the heart of Pakistani society. In September 2008, the Marriott Hotel in Islamabad was targeted, killing more than 50 victims and injuring many more. Violence by the Taliban and their affiliates has since spread to other parts of Punjab province. Then came the attack on Sri Lanka's cricket team in early March 2009 to the south in Lahore. The attack did much damage to Pakistan's image as a destination for foreign visitors and forced this year's Indian Premier League, a money-spinning cricket competition that attracts the world's top players, out to South Africa.

America under President Obama has abandoned the doctrine of overwhelming military force as the sole option to deal with the terrorist threat. His evolving policy is complex, more nuanced. It appears for now aimed at entering into a dialogue with sections of the Taliban in Pakistan and Afghanistan to isolate al Qaeda. It seems that the new administration accepts that America cannot impose its will and its own political system anywhere it chooses. It is not possible to transform traditional societies into modern ones all of a sudden. And Washington must have the "exit strategy," where it gets bogged down.

Therein lies the problem. To stabilize and to rebuild before exiting means to keep the military and civilian presence in Afghanistan, even increase it, for a while. It necessitates use of military power to control the campaign of violence by militants. Increased American and allied presence, military and civilian, provides the enemy with a greater number of targets. The result could be higher casualties. A determination made to keep the occupation finite involves negotiating with the adversary, and a deadline to expand the domain of constitutional order and peace. However, forces that are there in the region to restore order also provoke resistance. In Pakistan, America relies on attacks by unmanned aircraft against militants and Pakistan's security forces. Close secretive ties between Islamist groups and the military since the CIA proxy war against the Soviet Union in Afghanistan go back to the 1980s. These ties have proved impossible to break, despite persistent efforts of the United States.

A definite pattern appears to be taking shape. Every American missile which targets a suspected militant hideout reportedly kills some militants, but also civilians. Retaliation by the militants, a Taliban or allied group, follows. Can President Obama achieve what has been illusive for years? That is Obama's enigma.

ISRAEL ATTACKS GAZA AID FLOTILLA

May 31, 2010

It is inconceivable that the Israeli cabinet ordered the attack on the Gaza aid flotilla in international waters, killing and wounding scores of civilian passengers of dozens of nationalities without considering its consequences. Among the more than 600 passengers were people of all ages, Members of the European Parliament, United States and Israeli citizens. Turkey, from where the flotilla sailed, had said that the ships were indeed carrying humanitarian aid for the people of Gaza, where more than a million Palestinians have been under Israeli siege for three year.

According to Al Jazeera, the Turkish government summoned the Israeli ambassador to protest, and the Foreign Ministry in Ankara called it a gross violation of international law and warned of irrevocable consequences for bilateral relations. Angry demonstrations have been held in several places in Turkey. Condemnations of Israel are bound to continue in the coming weeks and months.

In the light of information widely available in advance, Israeli claims that the activists bringing aid were armed with guns and knives, and were Hamas affiliates who made attempts to lynch Israeli soldiers are grotesque. Equally bizarre is the Israeli military spokeswoman's claim that there is no humanitarian crisis in Gaza—claim that the United Nations relief agency and other humanitarian organizations flatly deny. Many people outside Israel will not believe these claims. An Al Jazeera correspondent traveling with the flotilla told the network that the organizers had instructed all the passengers to go inside the ship under attack and had raised the white flag.

The aid flotilla was at least 40 miles from Gaza in international waters. Some international lawyers are already describing the Israeli military operation as illegal, because the flotilla was on the high seas. As one of the ships was flying Turkey's flag, it was under Turkish jurisdiction. An Israeli radio commentator has suggested that the military miscalculated the strength of resistance from those on board. It must be said here that the passengers in international waters would have the right to defend themselves in the circumstances.

What does this episode tell us? It shows the Israeli government's determination to ensure that there are no more international attempts by activists to break the Gaza blockade in future. Even if future attempts were deterred, the international fallout of these events would be serious. From Jordan and Turkey to Spain and Sweden, many governments are joining in the condemnation of Israel. The latest episode is another severe blow against the Palestinian-Israeli peace process that was barely alive. It makes President Obama look powerless to influence events in the Middle East in any positive way. Many of Israel's critics may feel the aim of the attack on the aid flotilla was to sabotage the latest American attempts to resurrect talks with the Palestinian Authority.

As international criticisms grow, the Israel lobby in the United States and the Israeli government of Benjamin Netanyahu will intensify their efforts to counter them. Israel may continue to enjoy the protection of America's veto in the United Nations Security Council, but Israel stands more isolated now than it has been for many year in the wider community of nations.

LAW OF THE JUNGLE

January 24, 2011

Now this is the Law of the Jungle
—as old and as true as the sky;
And the Wolf that shall keep it may prosper,
but the Wolf that shall break it must die.

As the creeper that girdles the tree-trunk
the Law runneth forward and back
—For the strength of the Pack is the Wolf,
and the strength of the Wolf is the Pack.

—Rudyard Kipling, The Law of the Jungle, 1894

Tales of oppressors and oppressed abound in human folklore. According to one, there in the Valley of Outlaws was an unfortunate village traumatized by a marauder and a handful in his band. That democracy ruled the flock was their favorite boast and that no outsider was allowed to join them was their absolute insistence. The chief had long proclaimed that everything outside the flock was theirs—so God had willed, he claimed. Hence his men will take it all one by one. Armed with lethal weapons the marauding gang frequently attacked the village on the edge of the Valley. The raiders destroyed the villagers' crops, looted and burned their property, violated the dignity of women, did not spare children playing hide and seek in orchards. Drunk with power, carrying guns and swords, the band of outlaws inflicted a reign of terror on the villagers by day, even more by night. Those brave enough to complain and lucky enough to reach the powers that be promptly found the judge to be from the pack. The outcome was predictable, and the complainant had no chance.

Then there are episodes in recorded history that depict man's cruelty against fellow humans. Harvey Newbranch, in a powerful editorial published in the Omaha Evening World-Herald in 1920, decried the lynching of a black man outside the Douglas County Courthouse. "The lack of efficient government in Omaha, the lack of governmental foresight and sagacity and energy, made the exhibition possible," said Newbranch. "It was provided by a few hundred hoodlums, most of them mere boys, organized as the wolf-pack is organized, inflamed by the spirit of anarchy and license, of plunder and destruction." Further, Newbranch observed in his editorial, "Ten thousand or more good citizens, without leadership, without organization, without public authority that had made an effort to organize them for the anticipated emergency, were obliged to stand as onlookers, shamed in their hearts, and witness the hideous orgy of lawlessness."

The spirit of Newbranch's editorial rested in a sentence in which he said that "there is the rule of the jungle in this world, and there is the rule of law." We still live in a world where the rule of law is nothing but the rule of the jungle.

The report by Israel's Turkel Commission endorsing the Israeli attack on the Gaza-bound aid flotilla in international waters in May 2010 was entirely predictable. Prime Minister Benjamin Netanyahu appointed the Commission against worldwide protests two weeks after the killing of nine Turkish activists on board the lead ship the Mavi Marmara. The flotilla was on the open sea as it approached Gaza, its one-and-a-half million population living under an Israeli blockade. In setting up the Commission, the Israeli government rejected calls from the United Nations and governments for an international inquiry. The Commission's members were all Israeli, with two observers, the Northern Ireland Protestant politician David Trimble and Brigadier General Ken Watkin, former Judge Advocate General of the Canadian Forces. News organizations described them both as "friends of Israel." Even so, Trimble and Watkin had no right to vote on the Commission's conclusions, making the inquiry an all-Israeli affair. The inquiry was to look into a bloody event that occurred well outside the domain of Israeli law in

international waters. Still in Washington, officials of the Obama administration leapt to assert that Israel had the right and the competence to
hold such an inquest.

The Israeli government will feel that the Turkel report has served its
immediate need for a basis to counter the hostile world opinion. Prime
Minister Netanyahu will be relieved at Turkel's findings: the Israeli military's interception and capture of the vessels in the flotilla conformed
with international law; in most cases the use of force also complied
with international law; Israeli commandos acted professionally; and the
Israeli blockade of Gaza is legal; there is no violation of humanitarian
law. What else could Netanyahu have wished for?

Nonetheless glaring oddities haunt the credibility of Turkel and
Israel. Those who were traveling on the Mavi Marmara have numerous
accounts of brutality committed by Israeli commandos to tell. There
is enough film footage to reveal the behavior of Israeli soldiers during
the operation. Yet the Turkel inquiry was barred from questioning the
soldiers who took part in the operation, exposing its one-sided character.
Prime Minister Recep Tayyib Erdogan of Turkey has led the criticism
of the Turkel report saying it had "no value or credibility."

This is a return to the Law of the Jungle in the twenty-first century,
where might is right and attacking the young and the old, the frail
and the sick, male or female in open sea legal. Axes, clubs, iron bars,
slingshots and metal objects are weapons. "In the face of extensive and
anticipated violence," using one of the world's most advanced military
forces to neutralize activists—self-defense. The soldiers' conduct—professional and reasonable. Never mind worldwide condemnation. Law
is merely a tool. We are back to medieval barbarism where it is a crime
to be an underdog and the victim is responsible for what has happened.

WHEN NETANYAHU CROSSED THE LINE

February 19, 2012

The bombing of an Israeli embassy car in Delhi threatens India's diplomatic maneuvers between Israel and Iran, and has put India's discreetly nurtured ties with Israel since 1992 through a severe test. Those who are attracted to Israel's depiction of Iran as a terrorist threat to world peace would do well to read historian Mark Perry's account (Mondoweiss, February 17, 2012), revealing that Israel is recruiting, and collaborating with, terrorist groups in a secret war with Iran. That low-level conflict is spreading. Israel's latest reaction should be seen in the light of Perry's revelations.

The Israeli government's hasty and aggressive posture following the Delhi bombing has caused offense in the Indian capital. Officials in Delhi have made plain that India will not be recruited into the anti-Iran alliance under Israeli-U.S. pressure. India will not allow "Washington, the Jewish lobby and much of Europe to push the country into a corner" over Iran. How India conducts its ties with that country dating back to ancient times is its business. Furthermore, police investigations into the bombing cannot be rushed to suit external interests. The law of the land must take its course.

What particularly irked Indian officials was that immediately after the Delhi bomb (another device was defused by Georgian police in Tbilisi on the same day), Prime Minister Benjamin Netanyahu of Israel sought to upstage India's police investigations into the incident. Netanyahu described the Iranian government as the world's "largest terror exporter" and Hezbollah in Lebanon as Iran's "protégé." Foreign Minister Avigdor Lieberman went further saying, "We know exactly who is responsible for the attack and who planned it, and we're not going to take it lying down."

As if that was not enough. Israel's Energy and Water Resources Minister Uzi Landau intervened with his own comment, calling "India's support for the Palestinians at the UN a mistake," and that he intended to "persuade" the Indians to change their stand. And Israel reportedly asked India to help sponsor a resolution against Iran in the UN Security Council, of which India is an elected member at present.

A full-scale Israeli offensive to force a complete overhaul of Indian foreign policy was underway. In the unlikely scenario of it happening, such an event would be a geopolitical earthquake. India's reliance on oil producers who are firmly in the U.S. camp would be dangerously high. There would be other consequences in the short run. An audacious attack by Israel on Iran, with or without U.S. support, could be nearer, and so would the prospects of a wider Middle East conflict. India now stands between the present and the worst case scenario.

Police investigations were only beginning in Delhi when Israeli ministers spoke with such shocking certainly—the worst kind of megaphone diplomacy. For those sitting in the Indian capital, certain inferences were difficult to avoid. India had recently announced that it would abide by the UN sanctions against Iran, but would not obey additional sanctions imposed by the United States and the European Union. India would continue to buy oil from Iran, and an Indian trade delegation would visit Tehran in coming weeks.

Delhi was by no means alone in asserting an independent stance. Other countries, too, have been resisting what they consider to be strong-arm tactics by the anti-Iran bloc of nations to force reluctant governments to toe the line. The United States, the European Union and Israel are far from happy about this. That the affair threatened India's massive trade with Iran, and could derail India's capacity to formulate its foreign policy, was not lost in Delhi. A number of Indian politicians and senior officials made the government's position clear. Commerce Minister Anand Sharma said that terrorism and trade were "separate issues," and that business with Iran would continue. A former diplomat of India and now a leading commentator M. K. Bhadrakumar described the Israeli offensive as a "smear campaign" that "Tehran's agents had been going about placing bombs in New Delhi, Tbilisi and Bangkok."

Police investigations, and a visit by an Israeli Mossad team to Delhi, were continuing. Indian officials insisted that there was no "conclusive evidence" to link the attack to any particular group or country. And a senior police officer was categorical in saying that there was no link between the Delhi bomb and explosions that occurred in Bangkok the day after. The Indians are normally too polite to engage in crude public diplomacy, but when ministers of a country of under 8 million, albeit advanced and heavily militarized, try to dictate policy to a nation of more than a billion people, it is perhaps too much for the Indian sensitivities.

I am on record as saying that, in the challenging 1990s decade when the Soviet Union collapsed, India was hasty and ill-advised to build a "flyover" to Israel, and from Israel straight on to the United States. Over the years, Israel's multi-billion dollar sales of weapons based on American and Russian technologies, and intelligence sharing, have given India easy access to arms bazaar. But there is a cost. India can be vulnerable to pressure, and has ignored its interests in the Muslim world. Simply put, successive Indian governments put too many eggs in the (Israeli–U.S.) basket.

Now that India asserts its strategic interests independent of the United States and Israel, with the other members of the group called BRICS (Brazil, Russia, India, China, South Africa), it faces a trial of strength. The outcome will depend on whether Delhi can establish its capacity to turn away from what look like instant gains, and promises for future, to secure its long-term interests that are essential for India's place on the world stage.

POWER AND DELUSION OF GRANDEUR

March 19, 2012

First the video of United States Marines urinating on bodies of Afghans who had been killed. Then the revelation that copies of the Quran had been burned at Bagram Air Base, which also serves as an American prison camp in Afghanistan. Nearly 30 Afghans and several NATO troops died in the violent reaction. And as I mentioned in a column on March 4, the BBC Kabul correspondent described these events and the violent public reaction to them as the tipping point for NATO in the Afghan War.

Just as the U.S. commander Gen. John Allen and President Obama hoped that apologies from them would help calm the situation comes another disaster. If official accounts are to be believed, an American soldier left his base in the middle of the night, entered villagers' homes, woke up Afghan families from sleep and shot his victims in cold blood. After the killings, the soldier was reported to have turned himself up to U.S. commanders, and was flown out of the country. The accused has since been named as St. Sgt. Robert Bales. CBS News later quoted Bales' lawyer as saying that Bales "has an early memory of that evening and has a later of that, but he doesn't have memory in between." Other reports tell a different story, indicating that a group of soldiers was involved.

The massacre was committed in Kandahar, a province where NATO forces regularly carry out night raids on Afghan homes. They capture and kill men sweepingly described as Taliban, their supporters or sympathizers. Male family members leave their homes at night to escape foreign forces. This explains why 9 of the 16 murdered were children. The rest included at least four women, and five Afghans were wounded. Several bodies were burned.

The massacre of Kandahar has echoes of My Lai—a village in South Vietnam where American troops massacred unarmed civilians including women, children and old people almost exactly 44 years ago, on

March 16, 1968. The full horror of the My Lai massacre took time to surface, for many attempts were made to downplay it. Soldiers who had tried to stop the killings were denounced by U.S. Congressmen and received hate mail and death threats. It took 30 years before they were honored. Only one American soldier, Lieutenant William Calley, was punished. He spent just three years under house arrest, despite being given a life sentence.

The conduct of the U.S. authorities following the massacre of Afghans will be under critical scrutiny. Those who must bear ultimate responsibility will have to live with the guilt for years to come, and the carnage will continue to haunt the conscience of many people in America and elsewhere. The general sentiment in Afghanistan had already been turning dangerously hostile to foreign troops. Now, reports from Kabul say that Afghans "have run out of patience." In the midst of these events (U.S. Marines urinating on dead bodies in January, Quran burning in February, massacre in March), President Obama decided to invoke a comparison between himself and two of history's legendary figures, Mahatma Gandhi and Nelson Mandela. To me, the latest events in Afghanistan are dismaying, and the timing of the president's attempt to invoke parallels with Gandhi and Mandela is sickening. It goes to show what power does to its holder.

Much has been written about the New York fund-raiser, where President Obama gave his address as he sought support for a second term. I repeat the obvious to say that the country he leads has been engaged in a number of wars resulting in deaths and destruction on a vast scale. Their legacies will continue to take a heavy toll. Even when U.S. forces have withdrawn from occupied lands, or high-altitude bombing without deploying American troops on the ground has ceased, we will not know how long and in how many places Obama's secret wars are waged. In the November 2008 election, he had offered a hope of change for good. It remains as illusive as it was under his predecessor, George W. Bush.

Obama and NATO have moved and expanded the war theater—in Pakistan, Libya, Yemen, Syria, Kenya, Somalia and possibly places we are not aware of. His tactics have steadily become more threatening with foes and friends alike, linking ever more war and routine matters of international relations, trade and so forth. Despite the U.S. military withdrawal from Iraq and the Afghan project heading toward an end, there exists a more explosive situation from South Asia to North Africa. The scenario of a major war in the region haunts many. Obama may appear reluctant to attack Iran or Syria, but that clandestine warfare by major powers and their proxies continues is hardly in doubt. The Obama administration's aggressive, interventionist instinct is on open display. To draw parallels between himself and great souls such as Gandhi and Mandela is a grotesque parody of their historic struggles.

At the New York fund-raising event, Obama said that "the change we fought for in 2008 hasn't always happened as fast as we would have liked … real change, big change, is always hard." Next, making a leap into history, he continued, "Gandhi, Nelson Mandela—what they did was hard. It takes time. It takes more than a single term …"

Corruption infects our world in many forms: material and moral, visible and invisible, direct and indirect. But the underlying motive behind all things corrupt is a strong opportunistic instinct to benefit oneself at the cost of others by allurement or deception. No wonder politics has fallen so much into disrepute. The aphorism of the nineteenth-century English historian Lord Acton that "Power tends to corrupt, and absolute power corrupts absolutely" has acquired a special meaning.

Employing his political mantra of "change" and attempting to show likeness with Gandhi's and Mandela's life and achievements is one thing. Truth is a different matter. Gandhi never aspired for any political office, never held one, and did not fight any election. After his incarceration in prison for 27 years, Mandela was a reluctant president of South Africa, and made clear that he would serve only one term while a new generation of successors was groomed. Above all, Mandela used his presidency to avoid a bloodbath and stabilize the country as apartheid collapsed. Precisely for these reasons, both Gandhi and Mandela were such formidable opponents of the unequal and unjust systems which they fought.

Non-violence was Gandhi's tool. When violence erupted, Gandhi withdrew his movement against the British. He thought of others, Muslims and Untouchables he called Harijans (Children of God). He paid the ultimate price when a Hindu fundamentalist assassinated him in 1948. Neither Gandhi nor Mandela considered attacking another country, signing assassination orders, exaggerating or inventing facts about people they saw as adversaries. Mandela's African National Congress was inspired by Gandhi, but once the organization had realized that South Africa's vast black majority was up against an apartheid regime whose brutality was exceptional, the ANC did engage in a low-intensity war. The United States and Britain listed Mandela as a "terrorist."

President Obama recently justified his drone attacks inside Pakistan by saying that they "have not caused a huge number of civilian casualties." It is impossible not to interpret this as an admission that drones do kill and wound civilians. But it is a minor matter in the president's eyes. Only a few days ago, the German news magazine Der SPIEGEL said that while under the Bush presidency there was a drone attack every 47 days, the interval now under President Obama, the Nobel Peace Prize winner, is just four days. The Americans have "already executed 2,300 people in this manner." Nobody has a chance today if this president decides that their time is up.

Gandhi's agitation for boycott of British goods in favor of home-made products and his advocacy for an austere life were fundamental elements of the anti-globalization movement of his time. His ethos was "to consume less for the uplift of others from poverty and deprivation." He lived the life he preached, for which Winston Churchill, then leader of the Empire, disparagingly called him the "half naked fakir."

In the world ruled by President Obama today, Mahatma Gandhi and Nelson Mandela, were he not in his nineties and so frail, would be his greatest enemies. They could well have been on Obama's "kill list." Mercifully that is not the case, and this president can indulge in comfort.

Great people like Gandhi and Mandela use power to curb power. Barack Obama stands among those who use power to accumulate more of it. Therein lies the moral of any comparison in this debate.

CHAPTER EIGHT:

POWER AND MORALITY

On Power, Morality And Courage

November 27, 2011

For some time, I have been reflecting on the United States grand strategy anchored in the energy resources and Israel's defense in the Middle East. How that grand strategy, offering a validation for the Cold War in Asia and Africa, has lived on since the end of the Soviet threat two decades ago gives us plenty of food for thought.

Merciless continuation of that grand strategy meant the same old policies of propping up corrupt, repressive dictatorships, which at long last brought the Arab Spring in late 2010, and which is now a bitter and bloody winter. New retaliation by Egypt's ruling Military Council in recent days has created conditions for a second revolution in that country, whether it happens or not we do not know now.

The crowds at Tahrir Square are smaller than early this year. The Muslim Brotherhood, eyeing the parliamentary elections starting tomorrow, November 28, does not support the latest protests. The Brotherhood has calculated that it does not want to forego the opportunity offered by the coming elections, in which it is expected to do well. It also does not want to risk provoking Egypt's Military Council, and more importantly, the United States administration. For whatever reason, Brotherhood members seem to forget the history of the West using Islamists for narrow self-interests, then turning on former allies in the name of fighting extremism.

Nonetheless, the protesting crowds at Tahrir are ever more determined. With events threatening to slip out of control, the Obama administration again does not know how to deal with the crisis. America's current response is that "we condemn the excessive use of force by the police ... and urge the Egyptian government to exercise maximum restraint." With no warning or possibility of restricting American aid to Egypt's armed forces, this is the softest standard reaction from the U.S.

State Department to government onslaught on dissidents in a friendly country.

The latest events in Egypt, and violence and clampdown in Saudi Arabia and Yemen, have somewhat overshadowed the Western maneuverings in Syria and Iran, twin targets of America's grand strategy. A few days ago, STRATFOR published some additional context to events in the Middle East with reference to Syria and Iran, and explained reasons for escalated anxiety in Washington and friendly capitals with regard to Iran. Feeling misled when they supported the United Nations Security Council resolution for a "humanitarian intervention" in Libya, China and Russia will not repeat what they now regard as a mistake. NATO's conduct in the war in Libya has damaged, perhaps fatally, the future of humanitarian interventions with the Security Council's mandate. Hence Syria is unlikely to be Libya, with the United Nations acting as a tool. It partly explains reports in the region that France is training Syrian rebels to fight the regime of Bashar al-Assad.

The United States, Britain, Canada and France, all have increased the pressure on Iran in the last few days, superficially because of the "nuclear threat" which Tehran poses to the West's interests. In reality, the West's anxieties about Iran have far more to do with other events challenging America's grand strategy in the region. Washington alleges that Tehran's aim is to acquire the bomb, for which the evidence provided is thin, if not misleading and possibly false. Journalist Gareth Porter of the Inter-Press Service has disassembled the U.S.-backed case asserting that Iran is working on a nuclear weapons program. Porter's determined effort flatly contradicts the latest International Atomic Energy Agency report, which claims that Tehran might be developing nuclear weapons. In pointing the finger at Tehran, the IAEA director general Yukiya Amano, who had already committed himself to the United States, played a crucial role.

The New Yorker's investigative reporter Seymour Hersh, speaking on Democracy Now!, also described Amano's views as the "stuff of fantasyland." What happened with regard to Iraq in 2003 is now beginning to happen with regard to Iran. Following on his illustrious predecessors, Hans Blix and Mohammed El Baradei, Amano has not covered himself in glory, given that the IAEA report, prepared under his authority, has been so discredited.

The United States National Intelligence Estimate 2007 acknowledged that Tehran halted its nuclear weapons development effort in 2003, when America invaded Iraq. There has been no evidential change since, and Tehran continues to deny developing nuclear weapons. As the case against Iran is ceaselessly repeated in major media outlets, it is only right to state here that Iran denies it is trying to acquire nuclear weapons. In any case, it has a right to enrich uranium, within the framework of the Non-Proliferation Treaty, of which it is a signatory. On the contrary Israel, widely believed to be in possession of a substantial nuclear arsenal, would neither sign the NPT, nor would it submit its nuclear program to IAEA inspection.

Aggressive posturing by Israel and its allies in Washington, London and Paris against Iran and Syria runs the risk of persuading Tehran that it has no alternative but to manufacture the bomb one day. Should NATO's hawks and their Gulf allies succeed in toppling the Syrian regime, resulting in chaos and bloodbath, Iran's fears will only be heightened. The current game of brinkmanship leads to nowhere but the road to catastrophe. The cost will be high. Who will pay the price and whose interests will be served are the questions we must ask.

LEBANON, A VICTIM OF FOREIGN AMBITIONS

May 18, 2008

If you want to put out a fire, stop pouring oil on it. As George W. Bush prepared for his trip to the Middle East this week, he proclaimed that he was ready to pour weapons on yet another conflict.

It is Lebanon this time—a country that has in the past week suffered probably the worst sectarian violence since the end of the 15-year civil war in 1990. In an interview with the BBC, President Bush told the Prime Minister of Lebanon, Fouad Siniora, a Sunni Muslim, that "the United States is prepared to help strengthen the Lebanese army, so it can disarm Hezbollah"—the pro-Iranian Shi'a movement. Hezbollah has acted against its own people, Bush declared, and is destabilizing Lebanon. It is the latest among recent revelations about America arming one faction, only to use that faction to crush an adversary. Washington funds Sunni groups in Iraq, called Awakening Councils, to counter Sunni al Qaeda, as well as pro-Iran Shi'a groups. Other Sunni groups, including the influential Muslim Scholars' Association, have complained that Awakening Council militias are being used to weaken "legitimate resistance to American occupation." With U.S. help, these Sunni militias draw recruits from other resistance groups like the Iraqi wing of Hamas and the Islamic Army, which have turned against al Qaeda. They are also used to fight Shi'a militias that may or may not be allied to Tehran, but oppose the occupation of Iraq.

The U.S. Secretary of State, Condoleezza Rice, acknowledged in March 2008 that, in the Palestinian Territories, America armed the Fatah faction of President Mahmoud Abbas, specifically to drive out the democratically-elected Hamas administration. Rice asserted that the situation called for it. The American decision backfired, leading to the Hamas seizure of Gaza. The rise of the Taliban and al Qaeda is one of the outcomes of America's decision to supply billions of dollars worth of weapons to the Mujahideen to fight the Soviet Union in Afghanistan in the 1980s. President Ronald Reagan's decision gave America the victory over the Soviet Union in the Afghan war, after which the Soviet state collapsed. However, once the United States had walked away from the Afghan front, the Mujahideen and al Qaeda turned against America. The chaos of the Afghan civil war left in its wake an even more lethal phenomenon, the Taliban, who turned Afghanistan into a terrorist haven, from where al Qaeda planned the 9/11 attacks. Time and time again, Islamist groups which America helped with weapons and money to fight for its interests have turned on their masters. Does the current American administration not know history? Has George W. Bush not considered the possibility that the militias armed by the U.S. today could turn against it in future?

It is worth reminding ourselves about how the latest violence broke out in Lebanon. It started when the pro-U.S. government in Beirut, representing only a fraction of Lebanese society, tried to shut down Hezbollah's telecommunications network and remove the chief of security at Beirut airport, accusing him of being a Hezbollah sympathizer. Hezbollah responded by seizing control of West Beirut, crushing Sunni gunmen loyal to Prime Minister Siniora. A pro-government television news station was shut down and all roads to Beirut airport were closed. The fighting then spread north to the city of Tripoli.

These events have left the pro-U.S. Lebanese government humiliated and American policy there in disarray. Prime Minister Siniora knows the situation on the ground better than President Bush and has little appetite for conflict. Siniora was quick to announce that his government would never declare war against Hezbollah, and it was left to the wholly inadequate Lebanese national army to find a face-saving formula. The immediate confrontation subsided only when the army said the government orders to close the Hezbollah communications network and remove the chief of security at Beirut airport would not be carried out.

As the veteran British journalist, Robert Fisk, said in a report from Beirut in the Independent newspaper, this war is not about religion, but rather about the political legitimacy of the Lebanese government, which has a narrow base, and American support, which Iran challenges through Hezbollah. The truth on the ground is that Hezbollah is only one of many factions, albeit with considerable power and popularity,

in a country ravaged by internal conflict, fuelled by foreign intervention—not only by Iran and Syria, but also Saudi Arabia, Israel and the
United States. Lebanon is a theater of proxy war between regional and
international players, who manipulate Lebanese groups for their own
ends. In responding to current challenges, the Bush administration continues to use tactics that are dangerous today, and could create monsters
tomorrow. In Lebanon, as in the Afghanistan, Iraq and Palestine, the
focus should be on building state capacity—a difficult task, but one that
surely has more promise.

AL QAEDA DEFEAT: CLAIMS AND REALITY

June 7, 2008

Serious claims need serious thinking before they are made. The recent claim by the CIA Director, Michael Hayden, that al Qaeda had essentially been defeated in Iraq is astonishing. "Near strategic defeat of al Qaeda in Iraq, near strategic defeat in Saudi Arabia and significant setbacks globally" was Hayden's message in an interview published in the Washington Post on May 30, 2008. Was his message driven by evidence on the ground? Or was it a product of anxiety in Washington to point to a legacy before George W. Bush moves out of the White House?

The credibility of Hayden's claim was quickly shattered. On the same day, a suicide attack in the Iraqi city of Mosul, an al Qaeda stronghold, killed 16 people and wounded many more. Another suicide attack killed 10 people at a police checkpoint in Anbar province, west of Baghdad—a province hailed as a success story since 2007 for a sharp decline in the recorded number of terrorist attacks. Anbar is among Iraqi provinces where Sunni tribesmen under the banner of Awakening Councils are financed by the Bush administration, and armed, as a counter to al Qaeda. This American operation is no different in its design, explosive nature and future risks from the CIA operation to provide weapons and training to the Mujahideen in Afghanistan in the 1980s to fight the Soviet Union. Only this time, it might be easier for the Iraqi Sunni tribesmen, who are financed and armed with American help, to return to fellow-Arabs of al Qaeda or other anti-U.S. Sunni groups.

In Afghanistan, where Hayden claims al Qaeda is on the defensive, two NATO soldiers were killed in yet another attack, with several civilians hurt. In a subsequent attack, on June 2, 2008, in the heart of the Pakistani capital, Islamabad, about 10 people died outside the Danish embassy. There is little doubt that it was the work of al Qaeda, which had warned of retaliation against the republication of a cartoon of the Prophet Mohammad. In Iraq and Afghanistan, much is made in the international media of a sharp decrease in U.S. and NATO casualties, but something of a sinister nature is missed. The drop in foreign casualties does not necessarily reflect a drop in violence. The truth is that the Bush administration now fights proxy wars and uses national armies, as well as hired militias, to fight al Qaeda. When local people are put in front, they serve as shields that protect foreign occupation forces, at the cost of their own lives. I want to focus on Iraq now, because the invasion of that country in March 2003 has been the most serious failure and therefore the topic of the most upbeat claims by the Bush administration as it nears its end. Let us not play with semantics. What is really going on in Iraq is civil war under American occupation.

Two early decisions by Paul Bremer, the U.S. administrator appointed by President Bush, will forever be remembered as the trigger that brought a state of nature to Iraq, unleashing a war of all against all. By Order Number 1, issued on May 16, 2003, Bremer dissolved the Ba'ath Party at a stroke. With it formally collapsed the state structure that employed large numbers of Iraqis to run the country—both in the military and the civil service. In an article in Le Monde diplomatique in 2007, Toby Dodge, a British scholar, described the Iraqi population as dominated by a Hobbesian nightmare. He estimated that in the purge of the civil service, between 20,000 and 120,000 senior and middle-ranking highly-skilled officials lost their jobs. In the immediate aftermath of the fall of Saddam Hussein, as now, they would have constituted the very force to be used to restore order amid violence from insurgents and criminals, looting and anarchy.

In a subsequent move, Bremer issued Order Number 2, which dissolved the most important state institutions and their subordinates such as government ministries, Iraqi military and paramilitary organizations, the National Assembly, courts and emergency forces. To be prepared with alternatives to take over the functions of these organizations was essential in a country of 30 million people. The two edicts with no alternatives in place were a triumph of vindictiveness over rationalism. They caused the complete collapse of the Iraqi state's administrative and coercive capacity, leaving a vacuum that was rapidly filled by civil war. Iraq thus became a theater not only for America's war against terror, but a number of simultaneous conflicts, with rival forces terrorizing each other and millions of innocent victims in the country.

If only the President of the United States had gone into Afghanistan and concentrated on rebuilding the country properly instead of seeking to impose his vision of a modern, democratic state which is so unrealistic, and had continued to exercise non-military pressure on Iraq by international means, the prospects of a significant legacy of George W. Bush might have been infinitely brighter.

POLITICS, MORALITY AND THE GOP

September 7, 2008

The gloom of Hurricane Gustav was promptly blown away by the arrival of Sarah Palin, the running mate of John McCain, at the Republican Convention in St. Paul. The partisan delegates seemed genuinely thrilled by her acceptance speech, but last week's developments across the country remind me of an historic truth of politics. Almost 50 years ago, Harold Macmillan, then British prime minister, was asked what he thought was the greatest obstacle to political achievement. "Events, dear boy, events," came the reply from Macmillan. His words seem to have a powerful resonance in the U.S. presidential campaign today.

The manner of Palin's nomination and her galvanizing effect on the Republican faithful cannot be dismissed, but new revelations about herself and her family almost every day are impossible to ignore either. Some of these are acknowledged, others are contested. Complaints of exaggeration and distortion abound and threats of legal action fly. Republican advisors are irritated at the questions raised about Palin's selection by McCain, her qualifications and her views. In the face of persistent questioning by Justine Webb, the BBC Washington correspondent, a senior McCain advisor, Carly Fiorina, seemed angry, calling Palin's treatment by the media "sexist." With a Democratic presidential candidate of African descent and a female candidate for the vice presidency on the Republican side, race and gender cannot be far from debate.

It is the unexpected and unwanted events, which I referred to earlier, that represent "red lights" for the Republican campaign. As soon as McCain had announced his surprise choice of Sarah Palin as his vice-presidential running mate, the troopergate controversy blew up. It involves the dismissal of the Public Safety Commissioner, Walter Monegan, of the state of Alaska by Governor Palin. Was Monegan sacked because he was no good in the job? Or because of his reluctance to fire the Governor's ex-brother-in-law? On September 4, the Washington Post reported that it had seen an e-mail from Governor Palin, harshly criticizing Alaska state troopers for their failure to sack her former brother-in-law and ridiculing an investigation into her own conduct in the affair.

Then the announcement came that her teenage daughter was pregnant with her boyfriend. Palin is a strong advocate of sexual abstinence before marriage, so the episode was bound to pose a serious dilemma, as well as cause discomfort, for the Palin family. America is a country of fascinating contrasts. It is a nation where state and religion are supposed to remain separate, but religious and moral debate has acquired an increasingly important role in politics, most notably, though not exclusively, on the Republican side. The risks of this phenomenon are obvious. For those who fail to live by what they preach may be accused of inconsistency and hypocrisy.

It gets more embarrassing. According to the New York Times of September 3, Palin's husband, Todd, is a former member of the Alaska Independence Party—a party which wants to hold a referendum to secede from the United States. The newspaper quoted officials as saying that she had attended the party's conventions in 1994 and 2006.

As governor, she sent a video-taped message to the convention last year. How Palin's religious faith shaped her worldview was illustrated by an address she gave to a church gathering as recently as three months ago. She told the congregation that America sent troops to fight in the Iraq war on a "task that is from God." Imagine the effect of these words on the people of Iraq, where hundreds of thousands of men, women and children have perished for no fault of their own and millions have been displaced internally or gone into exile.

The Republican Party's counter-attack on the probing media has begun, but questions about Palin's past are unlikely to go away. The more appearances Palin makes on the campaign trail, the more interest there is going to be in her. And the more questions both McCain and Palin are going to face. From tabloids like the National Enquirer to highbrow papers such as the Washington Post and the New York Times, a range of news outlets have deployed extra staff. Alaska has become a favorite haunt for many reporters. The problem the Republicans face in this campaign is simple, yet considerable. There is so much interest in Governor Sarah Palin, because so little is known about her. It is a problem which is easy to understand, but difficult to tackle as "events" unfold.

I have witnessed political storms caused by events in my time. In his address to the Republican National Convention, John McCain ran through his military record, which thousands of party faithful applauded and more admire across America. As the speech went on, I heard the words "back to basics." They instantly reminded me of Britain in 1993. The government of Margaret Thatcher's successor, John Major, was weak and tired. Major was struggling with the grim state of the economy and social unrest. At a time of need for a huge investment of new ideas and money, the governing Conservative Party launched, perhaps fatally, the "Back to Basics" campaign. It was filled with high moral tone, at a time when the baggage of divisive, failing policies was heavy.

The campaign sparked intense public interest in the private lives of elected politicians in Britain. It was unfair to individuals, but the public interest was legitimate, precisely because it was an attempt to impose a set of rules on the vast majority of people that the imposers themselves did not respect. Exposé after exposé followed and powerful figures were forced to resign. The tide overwhelmed the Major government, ending in a resounding defeat in the 1997 general election—a humiliation from which the Conservative Party has only recently begun to recover.

There are episodes of history in America and elsewhere that mirror the fate of the Major government and shout out loud the lesson to be learned. When politicians bring prescriptive solutions to moral and ethical questions, they do it at their own peril. These questions are best left to the law and the courts.

ON MORAL CRISIS

May 13, 2009

The roots of violence:
wealth without work,
pleasure without conscience,
knowledge without character,
commerce without morality,
science without humanity,
worship without sacrifice,
politics without principles.

—Mahatma Gandhi

Rather like the state of the world today. We see violence in many forms, of which the latest is the scandal revealed of the "expenses bonanza" of British MPs using public money to maintain their own lifestyle. This at a time when millions of their fellow citizens struggle to cope with the economic meltdown. Ordinary people lose jobs, their homes, their possessions. Children go to bed hungry, their education suffers. After a long period of posturing by the rulers and their clamor to punish "benefit cheats," the day of reckoning has arrived. Britain's political parties are on the defensive not seen in living memory.

Recent disclosures in the Daily Telegraph newspaper make clear that the "benefit regime" for British MPs, under the rules which they themselves made, had been evolving for almost 30 years. Under the regime, large amounts of state money were claimed for gardening and for food. Private homes were frequently bought and sold, in one case three times in a single year, pocketing the money gained and avoiding the capital gains tax. Lavish furniture, clothes, pet food, bought at taxpayers' expense.

In one of the most outspoken attacks, former Archbishop of Canterbury, Lord Carey, condemned "the culture of abuse" and warned that
respect for parliament in Britain has reached a new low.

Of course, the crisis is more serious and widespread. "The culture
of abuse" in governance is both self-serving and self-perpetuating. It
shows malignant disregard for people outside the political bubble. The
attention of those outside the political bubble is often kept engaged with
endless talk of external threats like terrorism, evil dictators and illegal
immigrants trying to flood into "our country." Rulers may assume the
right to launch "pre-emptive attacks" that cause floods of refugees in
other parts of the world, but the refugees may not have the right to
asylum in the countries that cause the crises.

Warfare has become a business and an instrument to make enormous
amounts of money. For private firms like Blackwater in the United States,
combat in the battlefield, military training, consulting and personal
security for high-ranking officials—the list of what they would do for
inflated prices is long. In recent years, it has been official practice to
award contracts to firms of choice, without any real competition. Vested
interests prosper as a result.

Poverty is a form of violence. When an abusive culture has set in and
people in power have become comfortable in their own self-serving
environment, their interests fly against the needs of the wider society.
The consequence is more acute poverty, disruption and chaos. The cause
is rich feeding off poor. The effect a state of failure, as we see at present.

CHAPTER NINE:

THE ARAB AWAKENING

Egypt's Uprising

February 11, 2011

Day seventeen of the Egyptian people's uprising (February 10, 2011) brought a new dangerous twist to the crisis at the heart of the Middle East. Beleaguered President Hosni Mubarak gave a television address, but expectations that he would leave were once again dashed. He patronized the people, calling them his children; he apologized for the state-sponsored violence of recent days; he attacked foreign powers, clearly meaning the United States, for trying to dictate to Egypt; he asserted, denying an obvious reality, that he would never turn the country into a satellite; he would devolve some of the presidential powers to the longstanding intelligence chief and now vice president Omar Suleiman; however, he would not resign and would stay on until the end of his current term in September.

As he continued in this vein, determined to cling on to power, the popular mood of expectation turned into anger. People chanted "Go, Go, Go." Shoes were seen flying in air. It reminded me of a speech of Romania's dictator Nicolai Ceausescu in 1989. Before his fall, Ceausescu tried to address a crowd from the balcony of his palace, but the people booed him. Imagine if Mubarak tried to face the Egyptian people instead of addressing them on state television? What is surely the final phase of Mubarak's three-decade dictatorship reminds us of the most tumultuous events in recent history, reminiscent of the fall of the pro-U.S. Shah of Iran in 1979 and the fall of the Berlin Wall in 1989, symbolizing the end of the Soviet Empire and finally the collapse of the Soviet Union in 1991.

With popular rage sweeping the country, the pressure on the Mubarak regime, and uncertainty, were bound to increase. Friday would be another day of massive demonstrations. Already, labor unions, government employees, judges and medical staff had been joining the protestors. The trend was likely to grow, but Mubarak had failed to judge the nation's mood. Al Jazeera and Press TV reported about military officers at the Liberation Square in Cairo dropping their weapons and joining the demonstrators. The loyalties of Egypt's most important institution, the armed forces, to Mubarak and his regime look less certain. The game seems to be up. What legacy would Mubarak leave when he finally departs? For we are witnessing a phenomenon that is irreversible.

Egyptians living under a suppressive regime have broken the fear barrier. The masses have realized their collective strength and resolved to end their long nightmare. People have lived through atrocities and pain, economic and political hardships without any obvious recourse, distrust of their rulers and pessimism about their future long enough. They have reflected on what they must endure if things remained unchanged, examined their own worth and concluded that the system cheats them in every way. Their rage has broken the threshold of tolerance. They have decided that the existence of permanent humiliation is not worthy of continuation. The point of inevitability has been reached in the people's revolt in Egypt.

The inevitability of a revolution, once the dynamic has reached that point, is no longer in doubt. However, exact prophecy is trickier. Juan Cole warns against the temptation to compare Egypt's popular uprising to Iran's 1979 revolution (Why Egypt 2011 is not Iran 1979, Informed Comment, February 2, 2011). A number of observers have made alarmist predictions that the Muslim Brotherhood, with other radical Islamists, would take over power if Egypt's military-dominated regime is swept away by popular revolt. What a betrayal of eighty million people? There are secular, left-wing and right-wing parties, religious forces and labor activists in considerable numbers. Contrary to national elections and referendums to extend military-led rule under President Hosni Mubarak over three decades, the outcome of a free and fair election, if it were held, cannot be predetermined, nor can the general course of events.

Anti-Americanism in Egypt, the heart of the Arab world, is a different matter. Political machinations by the ruling elites in and outside Egypt to keep the established character of the regime in place will only serve to reinforce the anti-American feeling. Egypt's uprising has both differences from, and parallels with, earlier civil revolts elsewhere. The local context of the events in Egypt is different. However, it is important to recognize what these events mean for the United States, Israel and their strategic designs in the Middle East. They mean something akin to what the Iranian Revolution meant back in 1978-79. Mubarak's desperate attempts to cling on to power look similar to those of Iran's dictator, the shah, in his final days before he left the country in January 1979.

In the early stages of the Iranian Revolution, a weak American president Jimmy Carter in a moment of fatal misjudgment, described Iran as a "free country" and an "oasis of peace and stability." As the current Egyptian uprising started more than two weeks ago, the U.S. Secretary of State Hillary Clinton declared that the regime in Cairo was "stable." That only days after Clinton was moved to acknowledge the region being battered by a "perfect storm" demonstrated a crisis for Washington's understanding of the Middle East similar to the one three decades before. America's misjudgment and confusion about how to deal with the crisis does not stop there. The way ahead is littered with political landmines.

President Obama's soaring rhetoric proved much stronger than his leadership in office. He looks like a weak president in the mold of Jimmy Carter. In July 2009, he embarked on his Middle East political journey in Cairo with a celebrated speech seeking "a new beginning" with Muslims based on mutual interests and mutual respect, justice and tolerance. That rhetorical promise now faces a severe test. Obama seems clueless while American policy is hijacked by hawkish secretaries of state and defense, with the uniformed military top brass openly meddling in Egypt's affairs; and voices from the United States and Israel declare utter disrespect for the Egyptian people and the reasons for this uprising. Obama demands that a transition "must be quick, must be peaceful and must start now." President Mubarak refuses to resign, promises to go in September 2011 at the end of his current term (thirty years of rule in all) and offers instead committees to discuss reforms and bribes in the form of pay rises.

No matter what comes out of Egypt's tumultuous events, the United States' hegemony is facing unprecedented challenges. The Camp David Treaty that bought Egypt to the American camp for billions of dollars is in crisis. Israel, which has used Mubarak to maintain the blockade of Gaza and divisions in the Arab world, has every reason to be extremely worried. Autocratic ruling elites of other countries in the region—Jordan, Saudi Arabia, Syria, the smaller Gulf emirates and beyond—must be nervous. The Egyptian people have all but ensured the end of Hosni Mubarak's rule and the prospects of a Mubarak dynasty. However, this is only a partial victory. The real triumph will be the establishment of a true democracy in Egypt as its people demand. However, machinations in Israel, the United States and its European allies continue, and real triumph is not certain, yet. Is it to happen soon? Or the people's will to be thwarted, again? Attempts to cheat them this time will leave a legacy of anger and bitterness that will have consequences far more serious and long term than the events in Iran in 1979.

Mission Creep In Libya

April 23, 2011

Some commentators and politicians are describing it as mission creep—a slide into deeper military involvement in Libya, going beyond the original goal, and inviting unpredictable consequences. In simple terms, it is the decision by Britain, France and Italy to send military officers to organize the rebel campaign against Muammar Gaddafi. These "advisers" are being deployed mainly in the rebel stronghold, the eastern port city of Benghazi, to train and counsel the anti-Gaddafi forces, who have thus far not made much headway against the Libyan army, and have been beaten back in several places. Defense experts acknowledge that there will be more military personnel to protect these "advisers."

How does a humanitarian operation turn into "mission creep?" A brief look at events in little more than a month offers an answer. Resolution 1973 approved by the United Nations Security Council on March 17, 2011 authorized "all necessary measures ... to protect civilians and civilian-populated areas ... while excluding a foreign occupation force of any form on any part of Libyan territory." But any process of employing "all necessary measures" should begin with peaceful attempts. Otherwise, only military force has been employed. Indeed, the African Union had put forward a plan including these steps: an immediate ceasefire; unhindered delivery of humanitarian aid; the protection of foreign nationals; a dialogue between the government and rebels on a political settlement; and the suspension of NATO air raids. Furthermore, Turkey, a NATO member, had already begun to mediate between the two sides in Libya. But the West and the rebels insist that Gaddafi must go first.

Since the U.S.-led bombing of Libya started immediately after Resolution 1973, critics would be forgiven for concluding that the Security Council and Secretary General Ban Ki-moon have become tools of Prime Minister Cameron of Britain and President Sarkozy of France, with President Obama apparently dragging his feet. Ban Ki-moon, looking for another term as UN Secretary General, is culpable in what amounts to a Western attempt to invoke a seemingly justifiable humanitarian principle when, in reality, the intention of, and preparations for, a military assault were already in place. Any hope of a peaceful outcome stood no chance. Had the Obama administration, particularly his Secretary of State Hillary Clinton, acted a little more decisively in friendly countries, Bahrain and Yemen, when the rulers in those states were engaged in suppressing civilian protesters, the Western powers would have enjoyed the benefit of credibility on Libya. Gaddafi may well have seen a determined and consistent humanitarian policy on the part of the West.

Unfortunately, Britain and France have preferred military intervention all along. Cameron and Sarkozy are weak and unpopular men struggling with strong currents of domestic opposition to a range of economic and social policies of their governments. Every beleaguered leader knows that a crisis abroad helps to shore up support at home. What other reason could there be behind such zeal for another military adventure in Libya after the disastrous wars in Iraq, Afghanistan and Pakistan in the last decade?

In a boastful exclusive on April 20, 2011, Britain's Independent newspaper reported the deployment in Libya of "one of the most battle-hardened commanders in the British Army, with extensive experience in combat in Afghanistan." The Defence Ministry's message was "here comes Britain's own Rambo, fresh from Helmand." But those who have closely followed British military units in Basra in Iraq and Helmand in Afghanistan know that their achievements have been far from glorious, and the American military took over in both places. In the event of British, French or Italian casualties in the Libyan civil war, further escalation and deployment of troops is a possibility.

Even members of Prime Minister Cameron's own Conservative Party in Parliament are doubtful about the way the Libyan operation is proceeding. The House of Commons backed Security Council Resolution 1973, but John Baron, a Conservative, is among a number of parliamentarians strongly critical of the British Prime Minister, who wrote an article with President Obama and President Sarkozy, asserting that "Gaddafi must go, and go for good." Recalling that Parliament had "only given its backing for a no-fly zone to protect civilians," several MPs have accused the government of seeking "illegal" regime change in Libya.

Western claims that "Gaddafi is killing his own people" need an honest examination in the wider international context. War is a crime whenever and wherever civilians are killed and wounded. When peaceful protesters are killed or suppressed, it is an offense against humanity. When Gaddafi's troops kill civilians, it is a crime. Equally, when in Bahrain the ruling family's foreign mercenaries, and Saudi forces who have recently moved in, kill peaceful protesters demanding their basic rights, those troops are also committing a crime.

Violence against civilians in mosques and hospitals, denying treatment to the wounded, and threatening doctors, are among the worst of offenses. So is the violence against demonstrators by Yemeni government forces; killings by American drone attacks and death squads in Pakistan and Afghanistan; and the dreadful civilian casualties among the besieged Palestinian population in Israel's war on Gaza. Above all, the United States kills people, including its own, based on flawed justice, hunch, suspicion or whim. Unleashing brutal and blind terror is as much in the nature of civilized governments as it is of outlaw regimes.

THE FALL OF GADDAFI,

BEGINNING OF THE UNKNOWN

August 28, 2011

After sustained NATO bombing of Libya for five months, Colonel Muammar Gaddafi's rule is over. The fall of Gaddafi will be a welcome event to many, but Libya is no Tunisia or Egypt. Unlike Ben Ali and Hosni Mubarak, the collapse of Gaddafi's dictatorship is a result of massive military intervention. Two points should be made here. Libya is the second oil-rich state after Iraq to be a target of U.S.-led intervention since 2003. A small country of just over six million people, Libya is also endowed with vast high-quality oil reserves. Assuming authorization to "protect civilians" under a United Nations Security Council resolution in March, NATO flew nearly twenty thousand missions over Libya, including more than seven thousand bombing missions. NATO air power imposed a no-fly zone, and destroyed much of Gaddafi's air force, tanks, armored vehicles and heavy artillery in the initial phase of operations.

British, French and Italian special force were deployed as "advisers" in Libya, although foreign forces were forbidden under the Security Council resolution. NATO played a big role in helping the rebels storm Tripoli. Then, British and French personnel took on the job of guiding anti-Gaddafi fighters toward Sirte, his birthplace and last major stronghold. To insist, as NATO did, that regime change was not its objective is far from the truth. The international community, within the United Nations and without, did not have the appetite to send a peacekeeping force while the no-fly zone was enforced.

According to the most trustworthy data available (Guardian DATABLOG, May 22, 2011), nearly thirteen thousand military personnel across eighteen countries were involved in the operation, including eight thousand Americans. Weight of the conflict also fell upon Britain,

France, Italy and Canada, leading Western allies in America's militaristic foreign policy project, as well as Qatar and the United Arab Emirates. The British Prime Minister, David Cameron, was a leading advocate of intervention in Libya. He, with President Sarkozy and President Obama, will have to carry the responsibility for what happens in that country. Already, there are powerful critics of the path Cameron has chosen, not unlike that of his recent predecessor, Tony Blair, with George W. Bush.

As the Transitional National Council representing anti-Gaddafi forces issued statements about new Libya's constitutional shape, acts of looting were taking place in Tripoli, including Gaddafi's compound. Men were helping themselves with guns and reports of insecurity were emerging. Channel 4 News correspondent Alex Thomson's account from Tripoli's main hospital and mortuary gave a taste of things. Reports of revenge killings, acts of kidnapping and intimidation of foreigners abound.

In a country known for high-quality medical facilities, hospitals were full of wounded people. Shortages of food, water, fuel and medicines were acute, and there were electricity blackouts. It all reminded of Baghdad in 2003. The risk of the Libyan armed forces disintegrating must be high. The military and security services personnel, who fought on Gaddafi's side to the bitter end, and did not defect, owed everything to him. For them, defection to the anti-Gaddafi camp is not a safe option.

It is also important to note that many in the Transitional National Council are Gaddafi's ex-apparatchiks, including its leader Mustafa Abdul Jalil, who was his justice minister until a few months ago. Another prominent figure, Mahmoud Jibril, a U.S.-trained political scientist, was head of the National Economic Development Board in the Gaddafi regime before his defection. Western allies of the new power elite in Libya face an acute dilemma. To what extent will the culture of Gaddafi's successors be different? Will they be able to control the instinct of revenge and appreciate the difference between justice and vengeance? Will they be effective in restoring order in a country in which people are now extremely heavily armed? Will they unite Libyans?

Despite the TNC's claims of unity, Libya is a very diverse, and deeply split, country—a sparsely populated vast desert land. It has tribes; ethnic Arabs, Berbers and smaller African minorities, Tuareg and Tebu nomads; and opposing ideologies: Islamism, nationalism and Gaddafi's own brand of Arab socialism, though its time must be at an end. The celebratory mood in western capitals must not be allowed to overshadow a sense of foreboding and a desperate desire for a return to some sort of order. A failure of the Libya project is unlikely to absolve Cameron, Sarkozy and Obama of their responsibility by claiming that there were no foreign troops on the ground in that country.

THE KILLING OF MUAMMAR GADDAFI

October 24, 2011

Put your sword in its place, for all who take the sword will perish by the sword. This verse from the Bible speaks aloud of the manner of Muammar Gaddafi's regime, as well as his brutal killing. It is also a lesson for those who fought Gaddafi. The end of him has left a disturbing trail of savagery, from which the victors have not emerged unscathed. Where Western governments have been complicit and the mainstream media sadly restrained and unchallenging, Non-Governmental Organizations have strained their conscience and luck to speak against reprisals by both sides.

The Western powers are not in Libya as occupiers in a formal sense. That there are no "boots on the ground" is President Barack Obama's escape route. However, we know all too well that air power, especially drones, has changed the nature of warfare, making it possible to control territory from the sky. Boots not being there on the ground is irrelevant. Like the Northern Alliance in Afghanistan in October 2001, the Western powers have anti-Gaddafi fighters on the ground in Libya. In 1979, they had Mujahideen in Afghanistan, and the consequences are before us.

The United States, Britain and France, flying NATO's flag, embarked on a "humanitarian" bombing mission. Their remit, under United Nations Security Council Resolution 1973, was to protect civilians in Benghazi, initially by enforcing a no-fly zone. How different does that mission look eight months later? Only a few days ago, the U.S. Secretary of State, Hillary Clinton, visiting Libya, had said, "We hope he [Gaddafi] can be captured or killed soon." How many times have we heard the foreign minister of one country proclaiming that the leader of another be eliminated?

It was an act of incitement by an external power to anti-Gaddafi fighters to hunt him down. It was against United States law which prohibits state-sponsored assassinations, under a 1976 order signed by President

Gerald Ford. The order read: "No employee of the United States Government shall engage in, or conspire to engage in, political assassination." Further, it was against the Security Council's authorization for the Libyan mission.

Hillary Clinton's statement constitutes grounds for her, and possibly President Obama's, impeachment. But that will not happen under this Congress over a foreign war. Nonetheless, the assassination has ominous implications for the future. As Obama's reelection in November 2012 approaches, the appetite for war in Washington could turn out to be another blunder with a high price tag. Already, the International Crisis Group, a respected NGO, has warned of repercussions for Africa and of militant Islam.

Writing in the Guardian, the editor of London-based pan-Arab newspaper Al-Quds Al-Arabi, Abdel Bari Atwan, said, "Pictures of his final struggle will bolster those who remain Gaddafi loyalists—and make no mistake, there are many who will lament his demise, either out of self-interest or tribal loyalty."

What happened in the final moments of Gaddafi should be examined here. At the end of the battle for Sirte, NATO planes located a convoy of vehicles in which he was traveling. They bombed the vehicles, killing a large number of people. Gaddafi survived, but his brutal end was near. It is highly likely that NATO informed anti-Gaddafi fighters about his location. Images of his final moments leave no doubt that the 69-year-old former dictator was tortured by a frenzied mob before being killed. Among the crowds on Libya's streets these days are heavily armed teenagers willing to fight and kill. As the National Transitional Council celebrates "Liberation Day" today, what kind of Libya is in prospect must be a question that haunts not only that country, but the entire region. Meanwhile, the race for lucrative contracts for British companies there has begun. As Gaddafi's body lay in a meat store at Misrata, in London Defence Secretary Philip Hammond told British companies to "pack their suitcases" and head there to secure business.

Within minutes of the announcement of Gaddafi's death, leaders in London, Paris and Washington were hailing the event. Outside his official residence in Downing Street, British Prime Minister David Cameron declared that he was proud of Britain's role in Libya, and that "we should all remember Gaddafi's victims." Surely we should all remember those, too, who were rendered by the West to the Gaddafi regime to be tortured as part of the "war on terror." Cameron made no mention of them. President Sarkozy of France called Gaddafi's death a "major step forward." Employing his usual rhetoric, President Obama proclaimed that "the dark shadow of tyranny has been lifted." And Hillary Clinton shared a laugh on learning about Gaddafi's death. Her comment, "We came, we saw, he died."

Who will have the last laugh?

THE STRUGGLE FOR EGYPT'S SOUL

October 15, 2012

When the official announcement of Mohamed Morsi's election as Egypt's president was made following a tantalizing period of uncertainty, I had raised some questions about the country's constitutional future. I had also suggested that a multilayered conflict between the military and civilians, Islamists and secularists, conservatives and liberals was likely (Palestine Chronicle, July 3, 2012). An example of such conflict has been witnessed at Tahrir Square in recent days. Clashes between liberals and Muslim Brotherhood supporters show simmering discontent in a polarized society, as Morsi walks a political tightrope.

In his first hundred days in office, President Morsi has exercised caution, but also made some bold moves in a bid to keep many sides happy. On October 8, he announced a "blanket pardon" for all political prisoners, arrested since the beginning of the uprising which overthrew Hosni Mubarak in February 2011, and finally led to free elections in which Morsi won the presidency. The announcement said that all those serving prison sentences or still awaiting trial on charges to do with supporting the revolution would be released and charges against them would be dropped. The decree excludes those convicted of murder, but pointedly includes military officers arrested for taking part in demonstrations against Mubarak's dictatorship.

Pressure had been growing on Mubarak's successors to announce an amnesty, and Morsi could hardly have ignored it after his election as the candidate of the Freedom and Justice Party formed by the Muslim Brotherhood in the wake of the anti-Mubarak uprising. That he was careful to address wider sections of society, including the military, was no great surprise. The move was aimed at helping the new administration in several ways. For forty years under Hosni Mubarak's and his predecessor Anwar Sadat's rule, mostly with American support, Egypt's military-dominated ruling elite had alienated the opposition and much of Egyptian society. The new administration must demonstrate different priorities.

On closer scrutiny, however, his "blanket pardon" was described by some commentators as insufficient. The presidential decree's first article said that the pardon was "for all felony convictions and misdemeanor convictions or attempted crimes committed to support the revolution and the fulfillment of this goal." Amnesty International has now said that "all Egyptians tried in front of military courts need retrials, including those whose offenses did not relate to the revolution."

Morsi's political base is the Muslim Brotherhood, a major force in Egyptian society for decades. But his narrow victory in the 2012 election against Ahmed Shafik, the last prime minister of the Mubarak era and regarded as the military's favorite, was made possible with support from moderate and secular voters. Morsi cannot shake off the Muslim Brotherhood label, but he was careful enough to declare that he was going to represent all Egyptians.

The task of a president in post-Mubarak Egypt is extraordinarily delicate. He has to establish civilian control over the military, which has dominated the country's power structure for decades. Yet he has to work with the generals. He must not alienate other sections of the population even though he remains a Muslim Brotherhood figure above all. He must respond to raised expectations following the old regime's demise and his election. At the same time, he should ensure continuity and avoid a dramatic break from the past, for Egypt lives in a volatile environment.

President Morsi's move against the military top brass, particularly ordering the retirement of Field Marshal Mohamed Tantawi from his posts as commander of the armed forces and defense minister in August, seemed to have been executed with remarkable ease. But recent clashes at Tahrir Square highlight the continuing tensions between secularists and minorities on one hand, and Muslim Brotherhood supporters on the other. It is too soon to say that the task of reshaping the military into a force compliant to the democratically-elected government is complete. For the middle ranking and junior officers are bound to take longer to change. Meanwhile, the president needs their help to maintain order.

If Morsi's move to change the military's top leadership was executed with ease, his attempt to remove the state prosecutor general, Abdel

Meguid Mahmud, has run into difficulties. The president announced Mahmud's removal and appointment as Egypt's envoy to the Vatican after a court acquitted more than twenty senior Mubarak era officials of organizing an attack on protestors during the uprising. Mahmud's office was held responsible for presenting "weak evidence" against the accused, but the presidential order resulted in an outcry from the judges, who complained that Morsi had exceeded his powers in dismissing the state prosecutor general. In a setback to the president's authority, the prosecutor general said that he was going to stay in his job, and the president was forced to back down.

Another controversy is brewing over the draft constitution released for discussion. This time, Human Rights Watch has called on the Egyptian Constituent Assembly to "amend articles in the draft constitution that undermine human rights in post-Mubarak Egypt." The draft, it said, provides for some basic political and economic rights but falls far short of international law on women's and children's rights, freedom of religion and expression, and torture and trafficking. The fall of Hosni Mubarak was an historic victory for the people, but the outcome of the struggle for the soul of the Egyptian nation is far from certain.

Syria, A Middle East Powder Keg

July 29, 2012

In 1995, I had a rare opportunity to spend some time in Syria, where the Damascus Trade Fair was taking place. A normally secretive Arab country had opened its doors to a select group of Western journalists, businessmen and officials. The event was aimed at showing glimpses of a rich mix of civilizations going as far back as 10,000 BC, and described as a Hidden Pearl of the Orient. Syria today has Muslims, Shia and Sunni; Assyrian-Syriac Christians, ethnic Kurds and Turkmen in the north; Druze in the south. People of all ethnic and religious groups live in Aleppo, the country's most populated city. For centuries, Aleppo was the largest urban center in Greater Syria and the third largest in the Ottoman Empire, after Constantinople and Cairo.

Ancient Syria included today's Jordan, Lebanon and Israel. According to the Torah, on the other hand, God promised the "Land of Israel" to the Jewish people. And on the basis of scripture, the first Kingdom of Israel was established around the eleventh century B.C. Such ancient claims, religious or secular, are at the heart of Middle East politics, in particular the Arab-Israeli conflict. A civil war fuelled by foreign intervention has turned large parts of the country into ruins. Damascus is no longer the city where, despite a heavy presence of state security, Syrian families could be seen spending a moonlit evening on a picnic while children played hide and seek in the rocky terrain until well after midnight.

Like its neighbors Lebanon and Iraq above all, Syria has been fragile since the fall of the Ottoman Empire a century ago. All three states, and others, were artificially created amid the rubble of the Ottomans' Arabian domain, in a manner that split communities. The Druze, the Kurds and the Palestinians, each divided and enclosed in different national boundaries drawn by Britain and France under the legal instrument called "Mandate" are part of the legacy of the First World War.

My journey to Damascus in 1995 was by Air France, the only Western carrier flying to Syria at the time. It was a reminder that modern Syria and neighboring Lebanon were carved out by France under the French Mandate while Britain got the lion's share over Arabia, leading to the creation of Saudi Arabia, Iraq, Jordan and Palestine-Israel. The manner in which the modern Middle East was carved out by the victorious Allies after 1918, and individual territorial entities granted independence in subsequent decades, made sure that the new states were small, weak and unstable. It also made sure that those states could only be held together by authoritarian rulers, beholden to external powers. New imperialism was born and, like its previous incarnation, it was about controlling vital resources and trade.

Suspicion of Western powers, and of each other, in a highly diverse population runs deep in Syrian society, as it does in neighboring countries like Saudi Arabia and Iraq who aligned themselves to the United States or the Soviet Union during the Cold War. Syria remained the leading member of the "Rejectionist Front" for its determination of no-compromise with Israel and America over issues such as lost Arab territory and Palestine. The Ba'ath party, rooted in Arab nationalism, secularism and socialism, and dominated by military officers of the minority Alawi (Shia) sect, was as much a thorn in the side of the conservative Arab bloc as the West. The Soviet Union's demise in the early 1990s was a disaster for Syria. In the aftermath, Damascus did make attempts aimed at reconciliation with Israel, but failed. Syria sought compromises with the West, too, most shamefully in the rendition and torture of people in the "war on terror." It is mentioned in the Swiss senator Dick Marty's 2007 report for the Council of Europe and the European Parliamentary Assembly. All that failed to produce any concessions for Bashar al-Assad from Washington.

When I visited Syria in 1995, Bashar's father, Hafiz al-Assad, was still the country's president. I was among a small number of foreign journalists invited by Farouk al-Sharaa, then foreign minister, now vice president, to his residence in Damascus. I had taken a small tape recorder with me and, during our conversation over a cup of tea, I requested a short interview with him. In impeccable English, al-Sharaa declined. His response: "Syrians are not known for instant reactions."

The Syrians have long been suspicious of the West and its Arab allies while the West has consistently failed to read the country. These failures have been to the detriment of peace in the Middle East. For Syria is essential for peace and stability in the region—something that cannot be achieved by a Western-inspired overthrow of the present government in Damascus. The disintegration of Bashar al-Assad's government and Syria's armed forces will have disastrous consequences. With disparate groups in the population, and weapons aplenty in a volatile region, an Afghan-type scenario is very likely, and the consequences will be worse than those of recent wars.

CHAPTER TEN:

A NEW GREAT GAME

Georgia, A Pawn In Their Game

August 19, 2008

The conflict between Russia and the pro-U.S. regime of Georgia has been a decisive turning-point in Russia's relations with Washington and has taken us to the brink of a new Cold War. For the first time in almost twenty years, the West faces a resurgent Russia that has put the trauma of the breakup of the Soviet Union and the resulting chaos behind. Today's Russia is run by a younger leadership with autocratic efficiency, confident because of its vast energy resources and determined to resist American hegemony, by force if necessary. The crisis in Georgia goes beyond the Caucasus region. Its roots lie in America's overwhelming ambition to expand, and its tendency to make colossal miscalculations.

It is often said that the first casualty of war is truth. Behind the fog of disinformation coming from Washington, London, Tbilisi and, indeed, Moscow, the fact remains that the Russian invasion came after Georgia's bombardment of the breakaway region of South Ossetia. The vast majority of residents in the enclave are Russian citizens and Moscow had deployed its peacekeepers there. Many experts in Europe are depressed over the events in Georgia, and blame hardliners in the Bush administration for provoking the Georgian President, Mikheil Saakasvili, to adopt the aggressive posture that has brought this disaster.

What we see in Georgia is a classic proxy war between Russia and America, which has become heavily involved in the republic since a popular revolt in late 2003 ousted Eduard Shevardnadze from power, with Western help. Now, U.S. troops occupy Georgian military bases of the Soviet era, on the southern fringe of Russia. America provides weapons, training and intelligence to the Georgian armed forces. America's involvement, which began under the umbrella of the "war on terror" after September 11, 2001, has since become much more. If President Bush had his way, Georgia would be granted membership of NATO as part of the alliance's expansion around Russia.

The impoverished former Soviet republic is, in effect, a pawn in the broader U.S. design to encircle Russia. It is also located in a region which has some of the largest energy reserves in the world. For the Kremlin, the prospect of NATO coming so close to its southern borders is a step too far. Fortunately, some NATO members, most notably France and Germany, also do not see Georgia either as a full democracy or a stable country. And many in the alliance and the European Union have doubts about Saakasvili's ability to take mature decisions.

In an era when America has assumed the right to launch preemptive strikes, it is difficult to see the Kremlin behaving differently. The prospect of Georgia joining NATO, which might deploy nuclear weapons on Georgian territory, is simply not acceptable to Russia. Remember the Cuban missile crisis of 1962. At the time, Soviet nuclear missiles, deployed just 90 miles from the coast of Florida, brought America and the Soviet Union close to a disastrous war and the Soviets were forced to back down. Does the White House not know history? Or do the neoconservatives in the Bush administration not care?

Saakasvili's decision to order the bombardment of the Russian-majority South Ossetia gave the Kremlin a convenient cover to invade Georgia, just as the Bush administration had found it expedient to invade Iraq in March 2003 based on claims that Baghdad had weapons of mass destruction, which were never found. Russia is playing for bigger stakes now, just as America did in Iraq a few years ago.

About one-fifth of Georgia has fallen under Russian military occupation and the Kremlin leadership seems to be in no mood to entertain the idea of Georgia's territorial integrity in any negotiations sponsored by the West. There are daily condemnations of Moscow in the Western capitals, but the West is powerless to prevent the Russians.

This U.S.-Russia proxy war in the Caucasus has created a serious humanitarian crisis. President Saakasvili, Georgia's pro-U.S. leader, has been humiliated. Georgia's chances of joining NATO in the foreseeable future are negligible after the latest events. They have demonstrated that the West cannot and will not intervene militarily to protect Georgia from the Russian threat. The most important clause in the NATO constitution says that an attack on one member-state will be regarded as an attack on the whole alliance, which will use all possible means to protect the member-state under threat. NATO's inability to defend Georgia is a defeat for the West, and it is difficult to see how the alliance will accept the republic as a member.

The description by President Bush of the Russian action as "disproportionate and unacceptable" is laughable in the context of America's own conduct in its foreign wars. Washington should be more worried about the damage the crisis has done to its authority in the world. Diplomacy was never a strong point of the Bush administration. The blunders in Washington and Tbilisi have made the conduct of relations with Russia much more difficult. They may also have created other problems for the next occupant of the White House, for an increasing number of countries around the world may begin to look to Russia now that it has risen again.

Obama's Policy On China And Iran

July 20, 2012

Recent disturbances in Iran and China have drawn attention to not only the fragility of their socio-political systems, but also to contradictions in how the United States and other Western powers react to such events. America's response to demonstrations in Iran after the presidential election of June 12, 2009 has grown from one of caution to aggression and confrontation. On the contrary, its reaction over the outbreak of violence between Uighurs and Han Chinese in the far-flung region of Xinjiang in south-east China three weeks later has been one of timidity and silence.

Elections in Iran are not perfect, but China is worse for its citizens, its minorities in particular. The most contentious aspect of elections in Iran is the process of approval of candidates by the Guardian Council, a body dominated by the conservative clergy. That process having been completed, campaigning in the run up to polling had been remarkable. The U.S.-style television debates were notable for their sharp exchanges between candidates. All that changed after the authorities in Tehran announced the victory of President Mahmoud Ahmadinejad, the conservative incumbent, over his main rival, Mir-Hossein Mousavi, perceived as a relatively liberal figure in Iranian politics. The margin was overwhelming—63 percent for Ahmadinejad to 33 percent for Mousavi, his nearest rival.

While the Organization of Islamic Conference, Russia, China and India, among others, congratulated Ahmadinejad on his reelection, allegations of fraud were raised almost immediately in the United States, Britain and other European countries. President Obama appeared reluctant in the beginning to join in the chorus of protests from America's right. He even said that he did not want to be seen as interfering in another country's affairs.

America's political right and Israel lobby, represented by Republicans and Democrats alike, saw an opportunity. The Republican right, in particular, is keen to portray Obama as weak, just as it had done during the Clinton presidency. Obama's statement about "unclenched fist and extended hand of friendship," aimed precisely at countries like Iran, had triggered alarm bells among hawks on both sides. Senator John McCain, defeated by Obama a few months before, thundered on NBC's Today show, demanding that "Obama declare this a corrupt, fraud, sham of an election. The Iranian people have been deprived of their rights." After that intervention, voices against Iran became progressively shrill.

There are people close to the administration that believe Ahmadinejad actually won the election. The huge margin alone would make it difficult to fix the result in a country where the levels of education and political awareness are high. Time magazine on its website carried an article dated June 16, 2009; the headline was "Don't Assume Ahmadinejad Really Lost." The story, written by the magazine's intelligence columnist and former CIA field officer Robert Baer, made the point that demonstrations against the election result were held in north Tehran and in public places like Azadi Square, where the educated and wealthy live. These middle class liberals are among supporters of Mousavi, who say the election was stolen from him. Baer pointed out, however, that protests in poor slums and rural areas of Iran were almost absent. It is in these areas that support for Ahmadinejad is concentrated. However, such reports are inconvenient for anti-Iran hawks in Washington.

On July 5, Vice President Joe Biden sounded a strident note. In a long exchange on the ABC's television show, This Week, Biden's remarks were interpreted as showing the green-light to Israel's war-mongering Netanyahu government to do what it wants in relation to Iran. Asked whether the Obama administration would stand in the way in case Netanyahu decided that Iran posed a threat, and wanted to take out the nuclear program, Biden replied: "We cannot dictate to another sovereign nation what they can or cannot do." The most one-sided logic if there was one. Clearly, the principle of sovereignty applies to Israel, but not to Iran. Barely forty-eight hours had passed when Obama was forced to deny that there was any green-light from Washington to Israel to bomb Iran.

The Secretary of State, Hillary Clinton, was not going to be left behind in this game of aggressive posturing. On July 15, she warned Tehran that Washington's offer of "engagement" was not indefinite. Iran must respond now to overtures from Obama, or it could face more isolation. How can a U.S. politician known for her closeness to the Israel lobby, and who spoke of "obliterating Iran" during her failed presidential campaign in 2008, be trusted to want peace with Israel's main adversary in the Middle East? And how can condemnations of "election fraud" in Iran have any real effect from a country where, as many Iranians remember, Al Gore lost the presidency in the most bizarre circumstances to George W. Bush in the November 2000 election?

The events in Xinjiang highlight a deep festering crisis in a forgotten corner of China, where some of the most brutal tactics of suppression have been used by Beijing against the ethnic Uighurs, the Turkic Muslim community. Just like Tibet, large numbers of Han Chinese have been moved to the region, reducing the Uighur population to less than half. Xinjiang has seen several rebellions in the past. The toll in the latest violence is high—almost 200 dead, more than 1,700 injured and hundreds detained and tortured in one of the most remote parts of the world. The number of Uighurs leaving Xinjiang is in the thousands.

Despite all this, the response of the Obama administration, in particular of his Secretary of State, Hillary Clinton, continues to be minimalist and weak. The White House spokesman called for "restraint" by both sides—an odd attempt to strike a balance between China's rulers, whose treatment of dissidents and ethnic minorities has long been brutish and nasty, and a minority at the receiving end of the full force of the Chinese state. The contrast between Washington's attitudes to Iran and China underlines the vulnerability of the United States.

According to the U.S. Census Bureau, bilateral trade between China and America in 2008 was in excess of $300 billion. America owes China the largest public and private debt of around $2 trillion. And China is still useful as a counter to Russia. In an era of war-weariness and economic vulnerability, the Obama administration continues to show prudence without principle on the one hand and diplomacy without knowledge on the other.

A GREAT GAME IN ASIA-PACIFIC

April 30, 2012

India tested its first inter-continental ballistic missile, named Agni-V, this month, and joined the select group of nations possessing both nuclear weapons and a delivery system capable of hitting targets across continents. Only a few days before, nuclear capable North Korea had test fired a rocket, supposedly to place a satellite in the orbit, but it failed.

Within days, India's longtime adversary, Pakistan, tested a more advanced version of its Shaheen-1 missile. Named Shaheen-1A, it is capable of hitting targets between 2,000 and 3,000 miles—a substantially upgraded intermediate-range ballistic missile. Before the latest launch, Pakistan's longest-range missile, Shaheen II, was thought to have a range of less than 1,500 miles.

The North Korean attempt brought strong condemnation from the United States and its allies in Europe and the Asia-Pacific region. The Obama administration announced a ban on food aid to Communist North Korea, an ally of China. Pyongyang immediately said that it was no longer bound by the agreement to refrain from its nuclear program. The expectation in Washington is that North Korea will now conduct another rocket or even a nuclear test, its third since October 2006.

Reaction to India's first ICBM test was different from that after North Korea's unsuccessful rocket launch. The Indian missile is not something China can ignore. The Chinese are ahead of the Indians in the nuclear and space race by a decisive margin. Beijing has the capability of hitting targets anywhere in the world. It has had the atomic bomb since 1964 and the hydrogen bomb since 1967. It tested its first inter-continental ballistic missile four years later.

China's Don't Feng-41 missile has a range almost three times greater than the 3,500 mile range of India's latest missile. In all important respects, India is still in the Second Division of the nuclear league. Delhi hopes that further tests of Agni-V will enable the country to implement its nuclear deterrence in two years. Once the latest missiles are in operation, they will launch India into the First Division.

Notwithstanding the celebratory mood in India over the success of its missile test, the recent overall trend will be seen as an intensification of the arms race in the Asia-Pacific region. Whereas the North Korean nuclear and missile programs have caused upset in South Korea, Japan and Washington, India's Agni-V is unwelcome to China and Pakistan. It is hardly surprising that the Chinese response was filled with warning and ridicule. Pointing at its superior firepower, the Chinese media called Agni-V a "political missile"—and mocked it as being "dwarf." Beijing warned that "India should not overestimate its strength." And the Global Times accused "vested interests" of promoting an arms race between neighbors.

The United States reacted with an unusual degree of calm and understanding on India's entry into the league of nations possessing intercontinental ballistic missiles. President Obama had recently proclaimed the Asia-Pacific region as the new focus of American strategy, indicating it to be a logical necessity to depart from the grinding wars of the Bush administration and counter China and North Korea in the future. Reacting to the Agni-V's launch, a State Department spokesman called for "restrain" and, at the same time, praised India's solid "non-proliferation record."

With China continuing to build its naval and air presence in the Asia-Pacific region and beyond, and others striving to stay in the game, the race for influence among Asian powers is a reality. The West, led by the United States, eyes India as its long-term ally with a view to countering China. As the American administration continues its attempts to lure India into an ever closer alliance, Delhi is not wholly willing to oblige. Washington's offer to help India develop a "missile shield" is one significant issue between them. Then there are diverging views on relations with Iran causing tension between Delhi and Washington.

The arena of a new Great Game is Asia-Pacific. The race is complicated in a unipolar world, but the trend is clear. India's intention to close the gap with China is welcomed by the West in general and the United States in particular. Pakistan is determined to stay close to India's military might whereas China will want to maintain its supremacy.

WHEN CLOUDS APPEAR ...

January 8, 2012

When clouds appear, wise men put on their cloaks;
When great leaves fall, the winter is at hand;
When the sun sets, who doth not look for night?

—*William Shakespeare, Richard III*

The year gone by has been one of civil protests, upheavals and violence in many parts of the world. Old wars continued, most notably in Afghanistan and Iraq. Peaceful awakening movements that sprang up with much hope in Algeria and Tunisia turned violent as they spread east from North Africa to the Gulf region. A brief and bloody war in Libya, with an overt display of NATO's military power on behalf of the anti-Gaddafi forces, resulted in his overthrow and brutal killing. For NATO, the Libya war was over, but not for Libyans. A fledgling government now competes with warlords for territorial control and legitimacy in a fragmented society.

Talk of external intervention in Syria is loud internationally, but shrouded in secrecy on the ground. Accounts of the conflict are based on claims and counterclaims and not much independent evidence for corroboration. If detractors are to be believed, the Ba'athist regime of President Basher al-Assad is on the brink of collapse. The outcome of the Syrian conflict will have profound consequences in the Middle East, in particular for Syria's ally Iran, as well as in Lebanon and Palestine.

Human aspirations for liberty and freedom from oppression defined the year 2011. Paradoxically, great powers who played a role in sustaining oppressive systems, and still do where it suites them, declared themselves on the side of liberty in other places. The result is confusion, division, conflict, and a more insecure world. Afghanistan and Iraq in the last decade were America's "bleeding wounds," a term first coined by Mikhail Gorbachev in the 1980s Soviet war in Afghanistan. With both Iraq and Afghanistan far from stable, there is an unwelcome prospect of Libya and Syria also extracting a high price in terms of security threats and energy costs in the current decade.

Past events cannot be reversed, nor are their consequences easy to contain. So, I have in mind events which I believe the world in 2012 would be better off without. In the United States, from President Obama and administration hawks to his Republican opponents have been talking about punitive action against Iran and others in this election year. Powerful voices in the ruling circles of Israel, France and Britain are egging the American president on. The gap between rhetoric and posturing can lead to something far more serious. How civil movements can be manipulated by external forces for their own interests has been demonstrated during the current upheaval in the Arab world.

The overthrow and killing of Gaddafi may have resolved the conflict in Libya in the West's view. Now the prospect of real power remaining with the militias, and an ineffective Western-supported government, reminds one of Afghanistan following the 1992 collapse of the last Communist leader Najibullah. Libya, with its porous borders, surrounded by Tunisia, Algeria, Niger, Chad, Sudan and Egypt, is vulnerable itself and threatens others. The year 2012 could be decisive, not only for Libya, but for the region and beyond. The situation in Syria is extremely dangerous. Unlike Libya, Syrian state institutions are more robust. The regime's friends are not many, but Russia and China are taking a much tougher line with the West. Iran, its ruling allies in Iraq, and Lebanese and Palestinian groups have huge stakes in Syria. On the other hand, Saudi Arabia and Qatar, supported by the West, are determined to see the end of the current Syrian regime.

Turkey, a NATO member, has moved from its previous "independent" position to a stance much more in tune with the Western interests in the Middle East. Once a close ally of Syria, Turkey hosts the anti-Assad Free Syrian Army and allows the group to train its fighters and orchestrate attacks inside Syria. The Turkish military guards the Syrian rebel base, and a refugee camp, just across the Syrian border. For Turkey's governing Justice and Development Party, which professed to seek close relations with its neighbors, this is a complete about face. Two main factors appear to be at work. The Sunni support base of the party, and the prospect of joining the European Union—an idea that France and Germany in particular oppose.

How far Turkey's moderate Islamic government will go eventually is difficult to predict. It has its own Kurdish insurgency to contend with, so the risk is high. Turkey's growing involvement in Syria reminds one of the 1980s when, from a small beginning, Pakistan, in the midst of ethnic insurgencies, became a base for anti-Communist Afghan forces. The consequences were disastrous.

The conflict in Syria continues to simmer, and the sanctions on Iran are steadily being tightened. The talk of military action is persistent, and the risk of a weak U.S. president facing reelection being pushed into a war against Iran is haunting. Sectarian violence in Iraq is on the rise. The country faces a new political crisis after an arrest warrant was issued for the Sunni Vice-President Tariq al-Hashemi on terrorism charges, prompting the mainly Sunni party al-Iraqiya to boycott parliament. The Syrian conflict threatens further instability in Lebanon and the wider region. Between Libya in North Africa and Pakistan on the edge of South Asia lies an ominously explosive region, where the cycle of events threatens a catastrophe.

CONCLUSIONS

THE PROBLEM WITH AMERICA

May 15, 2008

The world has fallen out of love with the United States during the "war on terror" that started with President George W. Bush's declaration in the immediate wake of the September 11, 2001, attacks. Much of the sympathy and popular support witnessed after 9/11 have faded away, overtaken by stories about Guantanamo Bay, Abu Ghraib and extraordinary rendition. It is surprising how soon the goodwill capital, and a strong economy, can be squandered.

The events of 9/11 had forced the world into an extraordinary security environment. However, respect for the rule of law, the principle that an individual is innocent until proven guilty, and proportionality in the use of force were bound to become core issues for many people. America has long been admired as a land of freedom and opportunity, scientific and technological advances and its capacity to do good, but its policies have also generated strong opposition and apathy, creating waves of anti-Americanism.

What is wrong? The answer—the United States suffers from serious contractions between what it stands for, and its actions in three major areas.

Compulsive masculinity

The neoconservatives who came into the administration of President George W. Bush in January 2001 were staunch believers in America's military power and in using it to impose their will elsewhere in the world. America is a hyper-power, but its determination to rely primarily on its military power in the twenty-first century, well after the Soviet threat had vanished, has proved highly destructive.

The order ought be the reverse of it—soft power backed by the lawful use of hard power as the last resort. We have witnessed a damaging mismatch with regard to Afghanistan, Iraq, Iran, Syria and North Korea. And it has become obvious that even a hyper-power has its limits, and can overreach itself. There is loss of control that leads to hemorrhaging of political credibility and economic assets.

Gap between principles and conduct

Historically, America has stood for certain core values: democracy, individual freedom, human rights, open market and free trade. Inconsistencies are there in all administrations, but the problem became acute under the Bush administration, appearing to know only one way.

The neoconservative agenda was to impose democracy, but, as it turned out, only in those countries which they did not like. The list includes Afghanistan, Iraq and, if they had their way, Syria and Iran. What about Saudi Arabia—one of the most repressive countries in the world? The biggest base of al Qaeda is Saudi Arabia, but it is an ally and happily sells much of oil the industrialized countries need—so different rules apply.

The Bush administration kidnaps suspects from anywhere in the world, and sends them to detention centers like the one in Guantanamo Bay. There is no discussion of Saudi Arabia being a major hideout for active and potential al Qaeda members. Iran is reviled as one of the countries in the "axis of evil," for sponsoring terrorism and running a secret nuclear program. Iran does support militant groups abroad, but is not a leading backer of al Qaeda. The Bush administration tolerates lack of democratic rule, human rights and growing militancy in countries it likes, and saves criticisms and aggression for others.

When the burden of double standards becomes too heavy, erosion of moral and real authority follows. There has developed a wide gap between America's professed values and its conduct. The perception of double standards has never been stronger.

Difficulty in dealing with unpleasant legacies

The United States took more than two decades to come to terms with the experience of Vietnam. The process was helped by the ending of the Cold War. Now, dealing with the Iranian legacy is hard. It reminds Washington that the current ruling elite of Iran overthrew America's ally, the Pahlavi ruling family, in the 1970s. In a region of great strategic importance, Iran is a major regional power—its status enhanced, thanks to Washington's disastrous mistakes in Iraq. Iran is a difficult country to deal with, but the U.S. attitude is uncompromising, aggressive and unhelpful.

OBAMA, A COUNTER-REVOLUTIONARY

March 24, 2011

In my book Overcoming the Bush Legacy in Iraq and Afghanistan, I had described Barack Obama's victory over his Republican opponent John McCain in the November 2008 presidential election as a revolutionary event. Tens of millions of Americans, men and women young and old, lined up patiently to cast their ballots, in the hope of overturning the excesses of the George W. Bush presidency, and bringing a nightmarish episode in American history to an end. The American people had had enough of George W. Bush, one of the most unpopular presidents in history as he left office. He was despised abroad, wreaking enormous damage to America's moral and political leadership. An event by which the people constitutionally and peacefully voted to overturn the neoconservative Republican order under the Bush administration was nothing short of a "popular revolution."

Ordinary Americans in extraordinary numbers attested to the term "popular revolution" by donating modest amounts of money to the Obama campaign. Among them were low-paid workers, trade unionists, teachers and students. It was their "audacity of hope"—not so much Obama's—that gave them the belief that they could make the difference in a country tired of war and facing economic disaster. As Obama inched toward the Democratic nomination at the end of a bitter fight with Hillary Clinton, business magnates began to switch to the young pretender. Even then, support from the ordinary American accounted for more.

This widespread support at home, and goodwill abroad, was made possible due to Obama's promises of disengagement from the Iraq war, which he described as the "wrong war," (though the Afghan war was the "right war"), economic renaissance and setting aside "childish things." These promises he reaffirmed at his inauguration speech, and promised to begin a dialogue with the Muslim world based on "mutual interest and mutual respect." He devoted his celebrated, but soon to be outdated, speech to mending the broken fences with the Muslim world in June 2009. In sum, Obama promised to transform the way in which his administration would work, and eventually a transformation of the United States of America.

However, I also observed that I knew of no revolution that fulfilled all that it promised in the long run. I mentioned the Soviet Union and China in the last century; Cuba is another example. Countries from the Soviet Central Asia to Central Europe were released from the shackles of Soviet domination as Soviet Communism disintegrated. Two decades on, the situation in emerging states leaves a lot to be desired. Tajikistan, Kyrgyzstan, Uzbekistan, Kazakhstan are ruled with brute force by individuals or clans. Georgia, Poland, Romania are only slightly better. Other countries now firmly allied to the West have experienced racist authoritarian backlash.

Back to Obama's historic victory and the "popular revolution" it was in November 2008. It was the people's decisive response against George W. Bush's wars—in Iraq, Afghanistan and the "war on terror"—that provoked resentment and violent opposition, opened up sectarian divisions and created Hobbesian conditions of war of all against all. The consequences were taking an exceptionally high toll in economic, human and political terms. The people's mandate to Obama, the president, was to pull the United States out of the George W. Bush presidency's toxic legacy. A year after taking over the presidency, Barack Obama was demonstrating the first signs that a counterrevolution was underway.

Two years after, Barack Obama, once preacher of change and hope, has become a counterrevolutionary. His administration has quickly adopted the imperialist "Project for the New American Century" of the Bush era, discredited, despised and dangerous. He has shamefully gone back on his promise of closing down the Guantanamo Bay detention camp, hell on Earth made by torturers' infamy during the Bush administration. Obama has lifted the suspension on military trials of the remaining detainees, most of them innocent or forced to confess under torture, confessions that reputable courts would not admit as evidence. Reasons given by Obama apologists that the prison camp was not closed because the U.S. Congress did not cooperate are simply not good enough. Scores of Democrats in both houses of Congress were elected on Obama's coattail in November 2008, before the disaster struck the Democrats in the 2010 midterm elections. Where was his "Yes, we can!" rhetoric? Where was leadership? Guantanamo continues to be one of many blots on the United States of America. Compare Guantanamo to Castro's regime today on the same island of Cuba. It is Washington's shame.

Many more civilians, including women and children, continue to be massacred in Pakistan and Afghanistan in drone attacks that have escalated since Obama assumed the presidency. Unexplained killings of civilians and humiliation of night raids have proliferated. American death squads have massacred innocent civilians and kept their victims' body parts as trophies. The latest pictures, just a few of many, published in Germany's Spiegel are another bombshell. The Pentagon is once again "sorry." These pictures threaten damage to the Obama administration like the Abu Ghraib photos damaged the Bush administration.

Obama's promise of a dialogue with the Muslim world based on "mutual interest and mutual respect" has turned into an exercise in undisguised double standards no different from George W. Bush's. Obama's response to the people's nonviolent uprising in Egypt was slow. It was designed to ensure that, in the end, the Egyptian military remained in effective control, though Washington came to accept that it would have to abandon an old collaborator, President Hosni Mubarak. Even after the recent referendum, the situation in Egypt remains tenuous and prospects far from certain. Meanwhile the world's attention has moved elsewhere.

Libya has become Obama's first foreign military adventure, legal because it is based on a United Nations Security Council resolution, but questionable in its legitimacy, as several scholars of international law have pointed out. But double standards and callous disregard for human life and peoples' aspirations for freedom in Bahrain and Yemen are there to be seen. Secretaries of state and defense, Hillary Clinton and Robert Gates, along with U.S. generals, have hijacked foreign policy, taking the lead before cameras. President Obama these days looks ill at ease, his once soaring rhetoric having abandoned him. He presides over a counterrevolution that is a travesty of promises he made en route to the White House.

OBAMA'S SECOND TERM AND THE
MILLION DOLLAR QUESTION

November 14, 2012

The longest, most expensive elections in one of the most polarized democracies in the Western world are over. We now see contrasting reactions and unforeseen fallout—in the form of elation, bitter disappointment, investigation and resignation. The downfall of the CIA director David Petraeus and investigation into Gen. John Allen's emails concern both their personal conduct, as well as the uncomfortable fit between President Barack Obama and the conservative military hierarchy.

Nonetheless, the current turmoil at the top should not distract us from deeper analysis of American politics. The overwhelming nature of President Obama's win over his Republican rival Mitt Romney in the Electoral College was achieved by a series of narrow but even victories in hotly contested states. A win by a small margin in a state can deliver all of the Electoral College votes, so the outcome is distorted rather like in Britain's parliamentary elections, where a candidate can win by just one vote. It hides a greater truth—that the United States is a society split almost in two halves, as its demographic transformation continues.

The Republican Party's hysteria on a range of issues—from Muslims, Hispanics and other non-white communities to slogans of "small government" which threaten the vulnerable, low-income groups, women in particular—has damaged the social fabric of the United States and the party's own prospects. The trend is most conspicuous in the presidential and senatorial races, where constituencies are huge. However, it is not so accurately reflected in the House of Representatives, where the Republicans have maintained their majority. The omens for President Obama are hardly better in the second term. Fierce battles loom over the budget, with the Republican majority likely to do all it can to thwart the president's fiscal proposals, clouding his legacy.

The depth of polarization in American society is reflected in the overall vote. More than 90 percent of blacks and 70 percent of Hispanics and Asians supported Barack Obama. And 88 percent of those who voted for Mitt Romney were white. Yet, the difference in the popular vote between the two was smaller than three percent. How can these numbers explain Obama's solid victory over Romney and the Democratic majority in the Senate, but the Republican hold in the House? Is it because the ethnic (white–black), ideological (Republican–Democratic) and economic (rich–poor) divides are reflected in the smaller House districts more accurately? Is it because House districts are more definitely white or mixed, rich or poor, rightwing or moderate? In other words, has segregation—ethnic, economic, ideological—in the United States widened? Or have other factors been responsible for a very different outcome in the House? It is a topic for a whole new study.

Many of America's domestic afflictions remain as they were under President Obama's predecessor George W. Bush—possibly with two notable exceptions. One is Obama's rescue of the auto industry, the other his healthcare plan, which was compromised during the legislative passage. Its utility will be proven in time. Mitt Romney fatally damaged his presidential hopes by playing the politics of exclusion. Barack Obama helped his reelection by taking steps to rescue the U.S. auto industry, and delivering a healthcare plan despite disruptions and dilutions by his adversaries. The former contributed to his victory in the industrial states like Ohio, the latter in states like Florida with large numbers of Hispanic voters and pensioners worried about healthcare.

Now that the victory has been achieved, what are the prospects for President Obama's second term? I have alluded to the prospect of stalemate between the White House and Congress. The conservatives in the House showed dogged opposition to block Obama's healthcare plan, resist tax proposals and thwart his presidency in the first term. Obama's reelection has made the political right more bitter even as its support base shrinks. The real question is whether he will continue to be the compromiser-in-chief, reluctant to stand his ground and fight for the substance of his domestic program. Or his goal remains to ensure that the headlines show his presidency in good light, so he can leave a legacy of his choice, not necessarily much needed solutions to problems at home and abroad.

In foreign policy, Barack Obama did not take long following his inauguration in January 2009 to get back in tune with the past agenda, albeit with some adjustments, seeking U.S. hegemony over the globalized system. Initial promises of solving the Israel-Palestine dispute, rapprochement with Iran and the wider Muslim world and elimination of nuclear weapons were either diluted or abandoned or not heard again. Aspirations of a better U.S. human rights record were managed by silence, disingenuous definitions of combatant and civilian, and covert operations.

Withdrawal of American troops from Iraq was accompanied by the surge in Afghanistan—and those drones in the skies of Pakistan, Afghanistan and elsewhere. President Obama's announcement of a reduction in America's military presence in the Middle East actually meant a switch to increased reliance on special forces, drones and other mechanized tools of war, often deployed off-shore. A game of deception in the wider Middle East enables him to turn greater attention to encircling China. Will Obama's second term be very different from the first? Or will he continue to walk away from positions he appeared to take in the fist six months of his presidency in 2009? That is the million dollar question.

INDEX

A

B

C